Motivating Unwilling Learners in Further Education

Motivating Unwilling Learners in Further Education

The key to improving behaviour

Susan Wallace

BLOOMSBURY EDUCATION
AN IMPRINT OF BLOOMSBURY

LONDON OXFORD NEW YORK NEW DELHI SYDNEY

Bloomsbury Education
An imprint of Bloomsbury Publishing Plc

50 Bedford Square   1385 Broadway
London   New York
WC1B 3DP   NY 10018
UK   USA

www.bloomsbury.com

Bloomsbury is a registered trade mark of Bloomsbury Publishing Plc

First published 2017

British Library Cataloguing-in-Publication Data
A catalogue record for this book is available from the British Library.

ISBN:
PB 9781472942395
ePub 9781472942371
ePDF 9781472942401

Library of Congress Cataloging-in-Publication Data
A catalog record for this book is available from the Library of Congress.

10 9 8 7 6 5 4 3 2 1

Typeset by Newgen Knowledge Works (P) Ltd., Chennai, India
Printed and bound by CPI Group (UK) Ltd, Croydon, CR0 4YY

This book is produced using paper that is made from wood grown in managed,
sustainable forests. It is natural, renewable and recyclable. The logging and manufacturing
processes conform to the environmental regulations of the country of origin.

To view more of our titles please visit www.bloomsbury.com

Contents

Acknowledgments

Thank you to all the dedicated and talented teachers I've had the privilege to observe. And a thank you, too, of course, to those of their learners who provided them with every opportunity to demonstrate their very effective behaviour management skills!

Introduction

You walk into the classroom. Only half the class is there. Some haven't bothered taking off their coats and some are sitting with their back to you. They don't have any completed work to hand in. They're more interested in listening to each other than in listening to you. You find yourself addressing them over a background of constant talking, which forces you to raise your voice. The responses you do get are generally along the lines of: 'What do we have to do this for?' Or: 'Whatever'. Or: 'This is boring.' But you know it's not boring, because you've spent a long time preparing it and making it interesting. And you begin to feel your own motivation draining away, because you're only trying to help them, but it's like dragging a dead weight up a steep hill . . .

Sounds familiar? Further Education (FE) attracts many hard-working, well-motivated learners; but it also has its share of classes like this. And it's almost certain, if you teach in FE, that you'll have encountered one at some point. Some of the reasons for this – the systemic and societal ones – are beyond the individual teacher's remit to address; but the intention of this book is to focus on what we can do, within our classrooms and workshops, to get our learners motivated so that we and they can begin to fulfil our potential as teacher and learners. The worst possible response to the scenario you've just read is to assume that you're a 'bad' teacher or that they are 'bad' learners. Either of these assumptions presents us with a motivational dead end, as though that particular situation is inevitable and there's nothing we can do about it. Our own motivation and the motivation of our learners are to a very large extent mutually dependent. It's not just for the learners' sake that we want to get them motivated to attend, arrive on time, engage with the learning and hand work in; it's for our own sakes, too. Because motivating learners to learn is central to who we are and what we do as teachers, it becomes essential to our own motivation that we succeed in this. We all know it's never really enough to walk out at the end of a lesson knowing that all you've done is 'contain' the class but failed to spark the slightest flicker of enthusiasm. If we consider for a moment our own needs and aspirations, we'll all agree we feel much better motivated ourselves when we see our learners actually learning.

Practical strategies

This is a practical book. Although it identifies a range of motivational theories, its emphasis is very much on how to apply them in practice and how to evaluate what works and what doesn't. It takes as its first premise the idea that the FE teacher's prime objective is to encourage learners to learn, not simply to control their behaviour or babysit them or improve the college's retention and achievement figures – although all of these may also be a part of the teacher's role.

However, there's a second premise, which is that learners' lack of motivation is not always or necessarily the teacher's fault. In other words, there's nothing in this book to imply a deficiency model of the teacher. What it aims to do is to provide a sort of pooling of expertise by setting out some strategies and tactics that have worked for other teachers in a variety of situations. That's why you'll find all the discussion set firmly in the context of the FE classroom or workshop, and illustrated by realistic and recognisable examples of learners' behaviour and teachers' practice.

Barriers and strategies

The book identifies Four Big Barriers to motivation. They are Fear, Boredom, Previous Negative Experience and Lack of Hope, and we'll be looking at a whole range of tactics for tackling each of them. Set against them is another, more positive foursome: the four key strategies for motivating learners. They are Reward, Relationship, Respect and Razzmatazz. Each of these has its tactics, its advantages and its areas of minimum and maximum effectiveness. These approaches are demonstrated in the chapters by four teachers with very different styles. One is an expert in motivating through the use of reward; another bases his strategy on establishing positive relationships in his classes; the third one believes that to motivate learners she must first command their respect for herself and for the rules of the college; while the fourth gets her students motivated by making learning fun. Their names are Sly Cunningham, Davit Deera, Amy Harman and Loretta Starr, and of course they're caricatures really, each designed to typify a particular approach to motivating learners. They each have their successes; and, as you'll see, they also have their failures. But we can watch as, where one fails, another has a go, because obviously, as real-life teachers, we need to be able to use a combination of all these strategies if we're to succeed in motivating as many learners as possible.

We all know, however, that in the real world where FE teachers operate, there can be no blanket solutions to lack of learner motivation, and this book certainly doesn't pretend to present any all-purpose answers. In fact, you'll find it takes quite a pragmatic approach, acknowledging that there will be some learners whom you may never succeed in motivating. But they are a tiny minority, with whom the best you might achieve is to prevent them from undermining the motivation of the rest.

What you'll find in this book

The book is divided into seven main sections.

- First, it identifies the most common barriers to motivation and looks at strategies for overcoming each of them (Chapter 1).

- It goes on to explore four different approaches to motivation, looking at examples of how these work in practice, and listing some useful tactics (Chapters 2–5).

- Then it looks at ways to motivate individuals, particularly individuals who are undermining the motivation of the rest of the group (Chapter 6).

- The next section explores ways to motivate three specific groups: 14–16-year-olds in FE; adult learners; and school leavers required to re-take their English and maths qualifications (Chapters 7–9).

- The following chapter goes on to look at the impact of language on the motivation of learners: how to give effective instructions, what language to avoid, and the part body language can play in getting learners motivated (Chapter 10).

- The final chapter provides an opportunity to test yourself and your colleagues with a series of 'What would you do if. . .' scenarios (Chapter 11).

- Last of all, as a postscript to the book, we look at ways that you, the teacher, can keep yourself motivated (Chapter 12).

Why we call them 'learners'

You may feel the term 'learner' is being bandied about rather freely in this introduction, and, in the context of unmotivated students, somewhat inaccurately!

However, this is the term used throughout the book, in preference to 'student' or 'trainee' or 'group member', or any other term currently in use. This is not an arbitrary decision; the word 'learner' is used for a good reason. It describes what we're aiming for. It reminds us every time we see it used that our prime purpose as professionals is to help these people to learn and, if possible, to help them learn how to keep on learning. At the very best we want to motivate them to discover the satisfaction and enrichment to be gained from continuing to seek and develop new skills, ideas and knowledge. And at the very least we want to motivate them to become sufficiently proficient learners that they are able to proceed to the next step of their choice – whether it be a qualification, a job or progression to the next stage in their education or training. Regarding them as learners, and being seen to regard them as learners, is one of the first positive steps we can take towards motivating them to live up to that name. There's a bit of positive thinking at work here. If we think of them as learners, hopefully they will think of themselves that way, too. Our attitude towards them, and the way we express it, can be one of the biggest factors affecting their motivation.

In fact, the language that's used about learning in our classrooms and workshops can be a useful key to unlocking learners' motivation; it can certainly offer us clues as to why learners disengage themselves from the learning process in the first place. You can read more about the links between language and motivation in Chapter 10.

Establishing order

You'll find that here and there in the book there are places where tactics for motivating learners overlap with tactics for establishing orderly interaction in the classroom. This is inevitable, because if learners are to learn from you, they need to be able to hear what you're saying; if they're to learn positively from each other, they need to be able to work together without too much disruption. One of the keys to getting learners learning is to manage events so that they are interacting with you, the teacher, when you need them to, and not just with each other.

Sometimes just one learner's lack of motivation can eventually begin to undermine the motivation of others in the class, particularly where disruptive behaviour is involved. In an ideal world the teacher's recommendation would probably be that alternative provision be made for such a learner; but because the funding in FE is so often dependent on retention figures, this sort of sanction can be difficult to apply. This means that teachers sometimes find themselves trying to motivate the most unwilling of learners while at the same time doing their best to salvage and maintain the motivation of the rest. Two questions that this book frequently poses about the scenarios it presents are: 'Who needs motivating here?' and 'What is your priority in this situation?'

Groups and individuals

You'll find that the book takes a dual approach to addressing the problem of motivating learners. It looks at ways to motivate groups, and it looks at ways to motivate individuals. In Chapters 2 to 5 we see our four experts implementing their strategies with groups of unmotivated learners. Although they are successful overall, in every case there are individuals whom they fail to motivate. In Chapters 6 and 11 we revisit some of these individuals and see what happens when we try some alternative strategies.

Why motivation is a problem in Further Education

We might say that motivating learners is not a new problem, but in some ways it has become a more significant one. In the dim and distant past, the majority of FE learners could be reminded that hard work and successful completion would be likely to secure them a job in their chosen field. For those already employed, attending college on day release, there was the awareness that their employer had a vested interest in their achievement. Those were pretty good carrots. And the converse – fail your college course and you don't get/keep your job – was a pretty effective stick. We don't have recourse to that argument now, and it could be said that this makes the task of motivating our learners significantly more challenging.

Summary

This lack of external motivation forms part of the context in which this book sets out to share best practice and to offer you some useful strategies for encouraging learners to engage with the learning process.

This introduction has made the following key points:

- The FE teacher's prime objective is to encourage learners to learn.
- Learners' lack of motivation is not always or necessarily the teacher's fault, although it is his or her responsibility to address it.

- We need a combination of approaches if we're to motivate as many learners as possible.
- If we think of, and treat, learners as learners, they just might come to think of themselves that way.
- One of the keys to getting learners learning is managing events so that learners are interacting with you when necessary, and not just with each other.
- We feel much better motivated ourselves when we see our learners actually learning.

---

1 The Four Big Demotivators and how to beat them

Let's imagine a scene in your day; or perhaps it's a scene in your colleague's day. You walk into the classroom with your lesson plan and your handouts and your USB with your key point presentation on it... and there's no one there. About five minutes after the lesson's due to start, the learners begin drifting in – one or two, and then one or two more – until about half of those on the register have turned up. We're now fifteen minutes in and you decide to make a start. It takes several minutes to get them quiet enough to listen to you; even then a couple of them are still heads together, talking. You begin with a few questions, but there's only one learner answering. You suggest they take notes as they watch the PowerPoint, but you can see that nobody does. You ask them to get into groups and decide what the three main points were. As you move from group to group you find them discussing variously: what they did last night, nail extensions and *Celebrity Big Brother*. So you go to Plan B and get them together as a whole group and do some directed questioning. Shrugs, yawns and some laying of heads on desks. When someone's phone rings, several of the group express admiration for the ringtone. This is the most enthusiasm you've seen. You find yourself for a surreal moment wishing you were a telephone. At least that way you'd get their attention.

Do you recognise that? If you're teaching in FE it's almost certain that the answer's 'Yes'. You will surely have encountered a class like that one at some time or another. But let's just emphasise this point before we proceed: *many learners in FE are keen, well-motivated, hard-working and a pleasure to teach*. In fact, we could go further and say that most of them are. What concerns us as professionals is that a noticeable number of them aren't, and it's on those learners that we're going to be focusing our attention in the following chapters. A common assumption is that the learners who lack motivation are always the 14–19-year-olds; but while it's very often this age group who present us with the most difficulty when it comes to motivating them, adult learners can sometimes be lacking in motivation, too.

Why does this problem concern us so much? Why don't we just say, 'Tough! It's up to them. Why should I bang my head against a brick wall? I'm doing my best. If they won't engage with learning, that's their choice.'? I think one of the reasons most of us don't say this is because we understand our role as teacher to involve a sort of implicit contract between us and learners: that we'll direct and support them in attaining their designated goal – whether this is to gain a qualification, learn a skill, progress to a higher-level qualification or simply develop an on going appetite for learning. The trouble is, when we encounter a group like the one we've just looked at, we find we can't fulfil our side of the contract because the learners don't appear to recognise there's a contract there at all, let alone that it might call for some commitment on their part. This means we're thwarted in achieving our prime purpose as teachers, which is to help learners to learn. It wouldn't matter how much teaching was going on in that session; if there's no learning, then the teaching isn't achieving anything and is pointless. So let's make it our first rule of thumb. It goes like this:

Learning results from the joint efforts of teacher and learners.

We've all encountered learners who are under the impression that their learning is your responsibility, not theirs: 'You're the teacher. If I don't learn, it's your fault.' Such learners see their role as an entirely passive one. So what we're looking at here is how we can change attitudes in order to turn passive learners into active ones, and reluctant learners into willing (or even enthusiastic) ones. That's at the heart of what we mean when we talk about motivation. So let's create a second rule of thumb, which goes like this:

No amount of inspired teaching will add to a learner's knowledge or skills unless it also motivates him or her to learn.

In other words, the key to motivation lies in how we plan and present our lessons, and that includes how we present ourselves. So we've established from our opening scene that it's pretty easy to recognise when learners aren't motivated. But it's usually not so straightforward to work out why. Where did these people's motivation go? What's made them like this? Every parent or anyone with younger siblings is well aware of how full of curiosity children are; how they bombard us with questions: *'Why?' 'How?' 'Who?' 'What if. . . ?'* There's all that energy and joy they put into exploring and finding out about the world. Despite what we might think sometimes after a particularly bad day, our learners weren't born bored. Lack of motivation isn't hardwired in. On the contrary, the odds are there's an enquiring mind still in there somewhere; our challenge is to get them to use it.

But how? Recognising the problem doesn't necessarily help us know how to address it. It's a bit like going to the pharmacist and saying you've got stomach-ache. They won't know whether to recommend bicarbonate of soda or an ambulance until they have some idea of what might be causing it. So what sort of factors lie behind the disengaged attitude we've just been looking at? Well, first of all there are the socio-economic and cultural factors we mentioned in the introduction. In your role as FE teacher you're not going to be able to do a lot about those – nothing that will have an immediate blanket impact at any rate. But in order to make sense of our learners' attitudes and responses it's important that we keep in mind that wider context of pressures and possibilities that is shaping their values and aspirations. This is a context in which employment is not always easy to find; Higher Education is increasingly expensive, and the most popular aspiration is to be a celebrity – no qualifications required. So let's say in general terms that this is what we're contending with. But on the level of the individual student – on the level where we can make a difference – there is a range of factors that could be undermining motivation, and we need to be aware of them so that we know what we're dealing with.

The Four Big Demotivators

These are what we're up against. These are the Four Big Demotivators:

1 Fear

2 Boredom

3 Previous Negative Experience

4 Loss of Hope.

If we're going to deal with them effectively, we need to take a closer look at each one in turn, and see what's behind them.

1. Fear

Here are some of the things learners might be frightened of:

- you (yes, you, you scary person, you!)
- being ridiculed by the group for appearing clever
- being ridiculed by the group for appearing stupid
- discovering they're 'not clever enough' to do the work

- being ostracised by the group for breaking rank
- failure
- drawing any kind of attention to themselves in case they're asked to do something embarrassing, like read aloud (and remember that at certain ages just about everything can seem embarrassing).

2. Boredom

Here are some reasons they might be bored:

- The work is too easy and isn't challenging them.
- The work is too difficult and makes no sense to them.
- Other learners are causing disruption or slowing down the pace of the lesson.
- The topic is being taught in an unimaginative, tedious way.
- There's not enough learner activity built into the lesson plan.
- They've come to the end of their attention span (variously estimated at somewhere between five and 25 minutes, depending on the learner) and there hasn't been a change of activity/focus.
- The lesson is a long one with no breaks.
- They're not interested in the topic/subject and didn't really choose to be here in the first place.

3. Previous Negative Experience

Their experience of learning so far may have been a negative one and so:

- They come to lessons with no expectation of enjoyment.
- They see themselves as someone for whom education and/or training are irrelevant.
- They see you, the teacher, as The Enemy, and their disengagement is a form of sabotage or aggression.
- They've discovered in the past that 'winding up' the teacher is more fun – and an easier option – than getting down to some work.

- Their previous experience has given them the impression that education or training is about teaching rather than learning. Their learning is the teacher's responsibility, so as long as you're doing your bit, why should they have to bother?

4. Loss of Hope

They won't be motivated to engage with learning if they think they've no hope of:

- succeeding in the short term ('can't do this task')
- succeeding in the medium term ('won't get this qualification')
- succeeding in the long term ('never get a good job/income/photo on the front of Hello magazine, etc.')
- praise
- respect
- enjoyment.

Now, in reading through that lot you'll have spotted straight away that there are a number of things here that you can quite easily do something about once you know what the problem is. If you think back for a minute to the class we looked in on at the beginning of this chapter, it's quite sobering to think of the cocktail of demotivating factors that might be at work in there: learners who are scared, learners who are bored, learners who feel alienated from the learning process, learners who are hopeless – in more senses than one. And this is one of the problems of viewing groups of learners as an amorphous whole. Okay, so as a group they lack motivation; but as individuals they may lack it for different reasons. This means that a blanket approach won't always work. So what we need is a range of strategies and approaches that we can aim with precision, if necessary, at individual learners. And to do this we need to have some idea – as far as that's possible – of what it is that's driving individual behaviour. So there's a third rule of thumb:

Remember that even when a class of learners all appear unmotivated, their individual reasons for lacking motivation may differ.

Now let's have a look at some practical strategies we can use to address those Four Big Demotivators: Fear, Boredom, Previous Negative Experience and Loss of Hope.

1. Some practical strategies for dealing with Fear

There are plenty of things you can do (or avoid doing) to reduce learners' Fear levels. Some of these may seem more easily said than done; but in the chapters that follow we'll be looking in detail at how to make them work in practice. Here are a few of them:

- Be approachable.
- Demonstrate a sense of humour, but make sure if you aim it at anybody it's only at yourself.
- Don't publicly expose the weakness of any individual.
- Challenge the culture that derides 'cleverness' (see Chapter 10 for this).
- Start from where the learners are.
- Don't set them up to fail.
- Cultivate a sense of team in which the teacher and learners are 'us' rather than 'me and them'.
- Don't purposely embarrass anyone.

2. Some practical strategies for dealing with Boredom

As with Fear, Boredom can be tackled or avoided in a number of ways:

- Make good use of differentiation and individual learning plans so that learners are working to attainable targets that nevertheless offer some challenge.
- Identify those who want to work, and keep them engaged (we'll be looking at a number of different ways to do this).
- Be dynamic. Go for maximum impact. Surprise them.
- Don't always and all the time teach from the front.
- Plan your lesson so there's lots of learner activity.
- Build in frequent changes of activity or focus.
- Make sure you build in breaks.
- Discover what they're interested in, and start there.

3. Some practical strategies for dealing with Previous Negative Experience

Learners' Previous Negative Experiences are obviously not something you can do anything about; but if you suspect that's what might be at the bottom of the learners' lack of motivation, there are a few strategies you can try. For example:

- As far as it's possible to do so, make the learning enjoyable.

- Take every opportunity to encourage the learners to think of themselves as successful at learning (e.g. breaking down tasks into a number of smaller goals, so that the learner gets a repeated sense of achievement with each one).

- Avoid conflict and blame; emphasise that teacher and learner are a team.

- Don't allow yourself to be antagonised. Refuse to react to wind-ups. Use humour to deflect them.

- Plan your lessons in such a way as to discourage passive learning.

4. Some practical strategies for dealing with Loss of Hope

This is arguably the most difficult one of the Big Four. Restoring someone's hope in the future, short term or long term, is no mean achievement and succeeding in it is probably one of the greatest satisfactions you can get from your work in FE. These are some ways you might go about it:

- Plan your lessons so that tasks are broken down into doable steps that learners can have some hope of succeeding at.

- Take every opportunity to boost the learners' confidence.

- Praise learners whenever you can.

- Praise for effort, not just for achievement.

- Treat learners with respect. (In doing this you're modelling for them the behaviour you expect to see from them.)

- Act as though you enjoy teaching them (even if sometimes this is a tall order); plan your lesson to contain activities that are potentially enjoyable for the learners.

What these lists of possible strategies demonstrate is that you're by no means powerless to address the problem of unmotivated learners. In fact, with these lists, you can walk into any classroom or workshop and know you have a few tricks up your sleeve. But to say that there are things you can do to get learners motivated is not the same thing as saying that their lack of motivation must be your fault. You can't be held responsible for learners' previous experience of education, or for the level of job opportunities locally, or for the fact that their maths teacher mocked them in Year 9 and they've hated every teacher since (and *certainly* don't want to be doing maths ever again). So you don't necessarily have to take it personally and assume it reflects on your professional competence. You are, however, accountable for the planning of your lessons and for the way you relate to and communicate with the learners. In other words, there are things you can do something about and things you can't; it's the things *you* can do something about that we have to focus on here. This gives us two more rules of thumb:

> *Lack of motivation in the learners is not always your fault.*

> And:

> *When you recognise a lack of motivation in your learners you have a professional obligation to try to do something about it,* **as far as it is within your remit to do so**.

The important thing to remember here is that these two rules of thumb are not mutually contradictory.

How far can you go?

Before you begin spinning round like a Dalek, intoning: 'Motivate! Motivate! You will all be motivated!', let's make sure we're clear about the parameters of your responsibility. There are some obstacles to motivation that you can remove, some you can avoid, and some you can exterminate; and although at times it will feel as though you are working miracles, there are some demotivators that are beyond your remit or power to address. So let's finish off this chapter by establishing what objectives you might be able to accomplish in terms of your classroom practice, and what you almost certainly won't. The lists look something like this:

You can do something about. . .	You can't do much about. . .
• How you relate to your learners • How safe learners feel in your classes (from ridicule, sarcasm, embarrassment, bullying, failure) • Whether the outcomes you set for learners are within their ability to meet successfully, but not so easy as to present no challenge • Creating an environment in which motivated learners can concentrate on their work • Whether the lesson is presented in a way that will capture learners' interest and which involves them in active learning • How you design your lesson to be consistent with learners' attention span (assume 12 minutes) • Whether – if you do so – you're sufficiently selective to grab their attention well • Whether you provide breaks (even two-minute breaks where they don't leave their seats) • Whether it's more enjoyable, entertaining or otherwise rewarding for them to listen to you rather than to their mates • How you make the learners feel about themselves • How effectively you model good-humoured, respectful, positive interactions • How you help them define 'success' • How frequently you find (or make) opportunities to praise them	• Learners being on courses they didn't choose and for which they don't have the prerequisite skills (you can exert some pressure to get something done about this in the long term, but probably not to the immediate benefit of current cohorts) • Psychological, physical or social factors that undermine individual learners' motivation (although it's certainly part of your professional role to be alert for problems that might need referral for specialist help and advice) • Long-term demotivators, such as high levels of unemployment, which we might broadly term 'political issues'

Listing them like this is useful because it illustrates the fact that there really is a wide scope for positive action; the factors that lie beyond our immediate control are few by comparison.

Summary

In this chapter we have identified Four Big Demotivators: Fear, Boredom, Previous Negative Experience and Loss of Hope. We've looked at some strategies for dealing with these, and identified what is and what is not within the teacher's power or remit to address. To clarify this last point we've come up with five rules of thumb:

• Learning results from the joint efforts of teacher and learners.
• No amount of inspired teaching will add to a learner's knowledge or skills unless it also motivates him or her to learn.

- Remember that even when a class of learners all appear unmotivated, their individual reasons for lacking motivation may differ.
- Lack of motivation in the learners is not always your fault.
- When you recognise a lack of motivation in your learners you have a professional obligation to try to do something about it, **as far as it is within your remit to do so**.

2 Using Reward as a motivational strategy

Introduction

In the last chapter we looked at how an understanding of what's causing the learner's lack of motivation can provide clues about the best way to restore it. In this chapter we're going to take an alternative approach and look at how we can use one theory of motivation as our starting point. In the last chapter we got a glimpse of a group who appeared to be completely lacking in motivation. But if you thought they were bad, wait until you meet this next lot. Or it could be you've met them already. This is what their current teacher has to say about them. He normally teaches them first thing on a Wednesday morning, and he refers to them as. . .

The group from hell

Only about half of them ever turn up, and none of them ever get there on time. I don't rush to get there because there's no point hanging about for ten minutes waiting for them. I suppose you could say there's three groups really. There's what I'd call Harry's gang – about six of them – who seem to come along just to watch me and Harry fight it out, like it's a spectator sport, except they occasionally put the boot in too when it looks like he's winning. Most of the time they just snigger among themselves, or parrot what Harry says, or whoop and roar at his so-called jokes. Half of them sit with their back to me, anyway. That's them. Then there's another group – these are girls. They're a sort of loose alliance that's formed around a couple of strong characters: Kimberley and Meena. They make me the most uncomfortable. It's not that they're disruptive. They don't talk that much. They just sort of stare. I ask them a question and they just stare back at me. I ask them to get on with their work and they just stare. It's like they're daring me to push them too far or lose my temper. They also spend a lot of class time texting each other. But at least they're quiet. Meena really worries me. She just gets up to walk out and I ask her where she's going, and she says she's off to the toilet, but I know she's going off for a smoke because I always smell it on her when she comes back. But if I tell her to sit back down, if I tell her she can't go to the toilet, she claims she's got period pains. She complains loudly about it and starts to get quite graphic, so I always end up letting her go, just to shut her up. She does this every time. It can't be true every time. But what can I do? Kimberley's the one that's got a nasty temper on her, though. And it's completely unpredictable. Like yesterday I was just asking her to get on with some work, and she suddenly turns on me and starts shouting about how I'm picking on her and the lessons are boring and she doesn't want to be here anyway and I'm just a loser and I wear stupid sweaters and my breath stinks. And when I try to calm her down she just gets louder – and of course all the rest of them are loving it. Well, I say all the rest of them, but there's another, smaller group of girls who clearly don't enjoy this sort of thing. They always sit together, and they tend to be the target of snidey remarks from Kimberley and Meena's lot, so I think they're a bit nervous of them. I thought at first they were going to do quite well with their work, but they don't seem to have much appetite for it either these days. And then there's Neil – Harry's lot refer to him as 'Nelly' – who's actually very bright, in my opinion. He always turns up. He sits on his own. He never takes his coat off. He just puts his bag on the table and sits hunched over it the whole lesson. He'll always answer questions if I put them to him directly. But the other lads make this 'Oooooo!' sound every time he speaks, so I tend not to draw him in any more. I just pretend he's not there. It's to protect him, really.

Now, you're probably just itching to wade in there and put things right, so you might find it useful at this stage to make a list – on paper or in your head – of the ways that lack of motivation is manifesting itself in this group. You can compare your list with the one that follows in the next section. In a moment we're going to see what could happen if we send in a teacher to try out an approach based on popular motivation theory. We'll call the teacher Sly Cunningham. We'll be meeting him several times throughout this book. But before we see how he's going to handle this group, let's remind ourselves of the theory that will underline his strategies.

The behaviourist approach to motivation

If you ever watch those TV shows in which uncontrollable three-year-olds are taken in hand by an Experienced Nanny or a Wise Psychologist and within days – or sometimes even hours – are turned into happy, cooperative children, you may well have thought to yourself:'Hmm. That's all very well. But I'd like to see her try that with a bunch of the 16-year-olds I have to teach.' That's probably a fair comment. Dealing with motivation or behaviour on an individual level is a very different thing from trying to address it with a large, noisy (and sometimes threatening) group. Nevertheless, the same theories and principles can be applied, and often with great success. The strategies used by these TV nannies and psychologists are usually based on behaviourist theory. According to this, the most effective way to modify someone's behaviour is by rewarding them when they behave in the desired way, and punishing them – or, more accurately, withholding the reward – when they do not. This is popularly known as the Carrot and Stick approach. So the TV nanny may give the child lavish praise or a sheet of stickers for appropriate behaviour, but withhold the praise and prize – or even sit the child on the Naughty Step – when the behaviour is inappropriate. Consistently used, this approach motivates the child to behave in ways that are appropriate.

'Ah,' you may be thinking, 'the trouble with an FE college is that we don't have a Naughty Step; if we did, it would probably be too crowded with learners having a quick smoke or a can of drink before their next class to allow room for a few burly 17-year-olds to sit in disgrace.' Okay, so obviously the real reason we wouldn't use such an approach is that it would be entirely inappropriate to treat young adults in such a way. But this illustrates our dilemma. We know that a behaviourist approach can work very effectively when it comes to motivation, but how do we apply it in FE? How do we give or withhold reward? What sorts of carrots or sticks can we lay our hands on, and how do we use them? Let's see how Sly Cunningham approaches it.

Using and withholding reward

The next Wednesday when Sly takes the class he arrives at 8.55am to check out the classroom. While he's waiting for people to arrive he arranges the seating around the four large tables so that all the chairs face the front. He also writes this on the whiteboard:

There are four rules in this lesson:
Rule 1: We get a fifteen-minute break
Rule 2: We lose a minute off that break for every person who's late for the lesson
Rule 3: We also lose a minute from that break for every minute any one of you spends outside the classroom
Rule 4:

By 9.10am he has 12 learners present. They are asking him a lot of questions – about the rules, about where their regular teacher is. Some of their questions are rude and provocative. He responds to all of this with a slight smile, occasionally saying, 'Wait and see'. Because they haven't seen him before he has a certain curiosity value, and so when he does begin to speak he more or less has their full attention.

He introduces himself; he tells them he is delighted to be teaching them; and he asks them:

'Is there anything about those rules up there that you don't understand?'

The learners, who don't normally have a break in this session, understandably do have a lot of questions. While they are all shouting them out, Sly smiles and simply shakes his head. He holds up his hands to get them to damp down the volume a bit and says:

'I want you to raise your hand if you have a question you'd like me to answer.'

One of the girls raises her hand and asks how many minutes' break they'll actually get. Sly says they should, in fact, get only three minutes' break today as 12 people turned up late; but as they didn't know the rule beforehand he proposes that they start applying it from now on. Harry, who has not raised a hand, shouts repeatedly, 'What's number 4, then? What's number 4?' Sly ignores him and points beyond him to one of the quiet girls, who does have her hand in the air. She asks, 'What's Rule number 4?'

'The fourth rule,' says Sly, 'is one for us to decide together.' Harry is now shouting and jeering: 'Out of order! I asked that! I well hate f***ing rules anyway! They're f***ing stupid!' And so on. You get the picture. And his coterie are looking from him to Sly and back again with expressions of delight. Sly continues as though he can neither see Harry nor hear him. He says:

'So, people. What do you think that fourth rule ought to be?'

He only takes answers from people with their hand raised. The responses include all the predictable ones: finish early; don't have to do any work; be allowed to smoke in class. Kimberley's suggestion is that they should be allowed to use their phones in class.

'Ah,' says Sly. 'Phones. Kimberley, thank you for reminding me. There's already a college rule about phones. So obviously there'll also be a minute taken off the break every time a phone is used in class. And that includes the ringtone sounding. Thanks again, Kimberley. Well done.

'But,' and he produces a big bag of sweets and rattles it at them so that the inevitable outraged roar dies down a bit. 'But, I do have prizes here. And we're going to start with a prize for the first person who can suggest a Rule 4 we can all agree on.'

'Yeah,' says Harry sarcastically, 'like how about nobody should be allowed to take the piss.'

'Hey,' says Sly, addressing the class but not Harry, 'I've just heard a really good suggestion but I didn't see a hand up, so –' He shrugs regretfully.

Harry sighs heavily and raises a hand to shoulder height and repeats his suggestion. Obviously it's intended as a pointed comment on Sly's rule-making. But Sly responds with well-feigned delight.

'Excellent. That's great. Let's see if we can all agree on that one. And why don't we make it even stronger by saying something like: "We lose a minute off the break every time someone takes the piss or uses bullying or unkind behaviour." Let's take a vote. Who's for that one? Show of hands. Now.' A majority of hands goes up. Sly thanks Harry, praises him for coming up with such a good idea, and chucks him a couple of sweets. With the new rule written up on the board Sly now tells the class he's going to ask a few questions about the work they've covered so far this term. He'll accept answers from anyone who raises a hand. All correct answers get prizes. This goes quite well for a few minutes. Then Meena gets up and walks to the door with a packet of cigarettes in her hand.

'Don't be long,' says Sly. 'Don't forget, everyone's losing a minute off their break for every minute you're out there.'

'I need to go to the toilet, actually,' snaps Meena.

'We're taking a break in five minutes,' says Sly. 'At least, we will if you get back in time. So maybe you could wait till then?'

Most of the class weigh in at this point, telling Meena she ought to be able to wait five minutes. She gets very cross and storms out anyway. She's gone for six minutes. When she gets back the class has only a nine-minute break.

An analysis of the Reward/Sanction approach

Sly was faced here with a number of motivational issues to resolve. You might like to see how this list compares to the one you made after reading the first teacher's account of this class.

- punctuality
- lack of cooperation
- lack of interest in the work
- inappropriate behaviour
- bullying
- use of phones
- discouragement of willing learners
- Harry occupying the centre of the class's attention
- Meena's excursions
- Kimberley's outbursts.

Introducing rewards

Remember, Sly's approach depends upon giving and withholding rewards. As we've already discussed, the scope for doing this in an FE context appears to be quite limited. But, as you'll have seen, Sly solves this by introducing a set of rewards, which can be won or lost by the learners and which depend upon the decisions learners make about their own behaviour. Even more cunningly, he introduces a reward that depends not only on the learner's own behaviour, but also on that of others in the class: the newly introduced break. At the same time, he removes the factors that were encouraging unmotivated behaviour. We can summarise from this some rules of thumb:

- Introduce rewards that can be won or lost.

- Use the rewards to reinforce the behaviour you want to establish.

- Make some rewards dependent on whole-class response.

- Remove factors that reward or reinforce unmotivated behaviour.

Now let's look more closely at his tactics and at the thinking behind them.

Tactical use of reward	The thinking behind it
1. He arrives early.	The previous teacher had begun to 'reward' the lack of punctuality by tacitly accepting it and arriving late himself. Remember, if inappropriate behaviour is rewarded it will be reinforced.
2. He makes sure no one can sit with their back to him.	He needs eye-contact with all the learners so that: • he can reward responsive behaviour with praise that's directed at the individual; and • individuals are aware of when he's denying them his attention.
3. He writes up the rules.	For a noisy class this is the best way of getting their initial attention. It also 'rewards' them for reading the board because they learn something there that's interesting and to their benefit.
4. He introduces the possibility of a break that is contingent upon the learners' behaviour.	He now has a reward to give or withhold. He's also provided himself with a means of exerting peer pressure, so that the class dynamic might change from one of conflict (learner versus learner; learners versus teacher) to one of cooperation (notice his use of the word 'we'). He introduces Rule 3 as a strategy for using peer pressure to discourage Meena's cigarette breaks.
5. He leaves Rule 4 blank.	This provides him with another opportunity to reward the group (or at least appear to be rewarding them) by allowing them to decide one of the rules themselves. He later hijacks this shamelessly for his own ends but still manages to make it seem like a reward. He's not called Sly for nothing.

6. He ignores rude and provocative behaviour.	Attention of any kind can be construed as a reward. As long as there's no risk to Health and Safety, or infringement of college policy (e.g. on bullying or Equality and Diversity), he can choose not to reinforce undesirable behaviour by not paying it any attention whatsoever.
7. He tells them he's delighted to be there.	This is another way of demonstrating that they'll get no reward for rude and provocative behaviour, for example in terms of entertainment value by seeing him get wound up.
8. He begins with a question he knows they'll all want to respond to (at the very least they're going to want to know about Rule 4).	There's more going on here than immediately meets the eye. He's using their natural curiosity as a way of providing another means of reward; if they comply with the raised hand rule their curiosity will be satisfied. He opens with a question to which he's going to get a lot of response, thus bypassing the group's usual unresponsive attitude and denying them the opportunity to have their usual behaviour reinforced.
9. Before they can object about the second rule being unfair he beats them to it and says he won't enforce it retrospectively.	This gives the group the impression that they've gained something but without having to make a fuss or 'play up'. It creates the impression that they're getting a fair deal whereas in fact Sly's using it as a way of getting their implicit agreement that the rules will apply from now on. This tactic reinforces the idea of the rules as a way to gain reward (more minutes on your break) rather than as a punitive measure (loss of break time).
10. He tells them they'll decide the last rule together.	Again, this is presented as an example of fairness and negotiation, and as a reward to the group for entering into a productive dialogue with the teacher. In fact, Sly uses it as an opportunity to reinforce once again the raised hand rule.

11. He makes opportunistic use of Kimberley's suggestion about phones.	He uses this as an opportunity to reward Kimberley with praise for contributing to the group interaction; but at the same time he turns her suggestion on its head and uses it to tighten up the existing rules. In doing so he is also denying Kimberley the reward of 'winding him up', which is surely what she intended; and he is implicitly attributing responsibility to her for making the use or non-use of phones an additional source of penalty or reward. All this with a show of gratitude to Kimberley, who is being represented to the group here as aligning herself with the teacher.
12. He rewards cooperation and participation with sweets.	This provides a bit of fun as well as incentive. It reinforces the idea that attending the class and participating in the work can be enjoyable and far from boring.
13. He picks up on Harry's suggestion for Rule 4.	This tactic serves a number of ends. It allows Sly to: 1. demonstrate again to Harry that unacceptable behaviour and language will fail to gain him any attention 2. use Harry's desire for attention to lure him into complying with the raised hand rule 3. demonstrate to the rest of the group that this teacher can get Harry to comply and to contribute positively 4. hijack Harry's suggestion – which was clearly intended to be seen as a bit of bravado and a criticism of Sly – and wilfully misinterpret it for his own purposes. Thus he presents Harry, the erstwhile loudmouth and bully, to the group in a new guise. This reconstructed Harry is someone who's opposed to bullying or even raising a laugh at others' expense.

14. He assesses their current level of knowledge by asking questions and rewarding correct answers with sweets.	This is the first time we see Sly focusing on the subject he's teaching. Until now he's been establishing ground rules, using reward to gain the group's cooperation. The success of this next step (that is, all learners participating, not shouting out, enjoying the lesson) wouldn't have been possible without the ground-gaining tactics he's already employed. It's allowed him to move into a subject-based question-and-answer session with a cooperative and apparently motivated class.
15. When Meena walks to the door, Sly attempts to apply peer pressure on her to remain in class another five minutes until the break.	He's set this tactic up well, and it deserves to succeed. But it doesn't. Meena's need for a cigarette proves more powerful than her need for peer approval. Or perhaps there's more to it than that? In any event, Sly didn't succeed in motivating Meena to stay. But then you can't win them all.

Questionable tactics?

There may be some aspects of Sly's approach that you would want to question. Look at that scenario again and consider how you feel, for example, about:

- his use of sweets as a reward (does this appear to infantilise the learners?)

- his insistence that they raise their hand if they want to be heard (how appropriate is that for this age-group?)

- his 'setting up' of Kimberley to be the target of peer resentment

- his exposure of Meena to peer pressure

- his assumption that her only problem is nicotine addiction

- his sleight of hand about the mobile phone rule

- his appropriation of Rule 4 under the guise of democratic decision-making.

If any of these, or anything else he did, seems to you to be questionable, then you will exercise your professional judgement about whether or not you want to use them as examples to follow, just as Sly has used his own professional judgement in choosing to employ these tactics in the first place. If it was against college policy to allow learners a mid-lesson break, an alternative reward in that case could be the lure of having music playing while the class is working, for example.

What we don't see here is how this approach works out in the long term. Does the learners' punctuality improve? Does he eventually succeed with Meena? Do his tactics succeed in making Neil feel comfortable within the group, and do they provide an opportunity for the 'quiet group' to regain their enthusiasm for learning? We'll be meeting Sly Cunningham again later in the book to see how his work with this group is progressing.

Summary

In this chapter we've explored how opportunities can be created to use reward and the withholding of reward in order to motivate learners in FE. The tactics we've discussed can be summarised in the following way:

- Introduce rewards that can be won. . . or lost.
- Use the rewards to reinforce the behaviour you want to establish.
- Make some rewards dependent on whole-class response.
- Remove factors that reward or reinforce disengaged and unmotivated behaviour.

There has been some mention of 'sticks' and 'carrots' in this chapter. In Chapter 10 you'll find a discussion of this sort of language and its implications for our interactions with unmotivated learners.

3 Building motivation through positive Relationships

In the previous chapter we looked at how we could use Reward to improve the motivation of learners. In this chapter we're going to focus on a different strategy; we're going to explore the ways in which Relationships in the classroom or workshop can be used to improve learner motivation. We're also going to argue that the responsibility for building a positive and constructive Relationship lies firmly with the teacher, who may sometimes have to persevere for some time in the face of seemingly impossible odds. However, while this is perhaps the most difficult strategy to establish and to implement consistently, it is also arguably the most potentially powerful.

Even though we're talking about interactions and relationships here, we have to recognise that in a sense all motivation is reward-driven. The idea of a reward or pay-off of some kind is implicit in the very word 'motivation', so that when we talk about being motivated, we're normally talking about aiming to achieve or do something, with a particular reward or goal in mind. Even when we describe someone as a 'motivated person' there's still an implied goal, even if it's an abstract one, like 'success' or 'knowledge'. However, there's clearly a difference between a learner being motivated by the promise of sweets and a learner being motivated by a desire for knowledge or success. In the first case the source of motivation is the teacher, while in the second the motivation comes from within the learners themselves. And similarly, in the first the goal has been chosen by the teacher (e.g. getting the learners to complete an assignment task), while in the second the goal is one the learners have chosen for themselves.

Extrinsic and intrinsic motivation

We can refer to the promise of prizes such as jobs and sweets and stickers as examples of *extrinsic* motivation, motivation that's based on the hope of an externally offered reward. The other type of motivation we refer to as *intrinsic* motivation. This is the motivation that comes from within and forms part of the learner's attitude to life, learning and work. We see it in learners who enjoy learning and seem to view the achievement of knowledge and skills, at least in part, as its own reward. If all our learners were intrinsically motivated, I wouldn't be writing this book and you wouldn't be reading it.

The group that don't care

So imagine this. You arrive to do a peer observation of a colleague who's teaching a class you've never met before. You arrive a few minutes after the lesson is due to start and this is what you find.

The teacher is struggling to make her voice heard above the learners' loud comments and conversation. She seems to be asking for assignments to be handed in, but no one's taking any notice. She keeps shouting, 'Er, keep it down, please!' and 'Are you listening? You need to listen to this!' But it's having no effect. Eventually she starts going up to the learners table by table and asking for their assignments. It's difficult for you to hear what they're saying, but it's clear no one has brought any work to hand in. The teacher's obviously getting increasingly cross, and the noise level is steadily rising, until suddenly she storms back to her table, turns to the class and shouts: 'Look! I've had enough of you lot! Just SHUT UP!!' There's some shock value to this, and it creates a temporary lull in which the learners are able to clearly hear what she says next. 'I'm sick and tired of wasting my time with you. You're all a complete waste of space. I don't know why you're here. And if you can't be bothered to do any of your assignments then I just couldn't care less.' There's a moment's surprised silence, and then one of the learners says, in a mock-camp voice, 'Oooooo!' and the whole group erupts into laughter. The teacher points a finger at two of the noisiest – a couple of lads who are sitting near the back. 'You two. Get up here and sit at the front where I can see you.' The two she's picked on object that this is 'well out of order', but nevertheless comply, dumping their sports bags on the table immediately in front of the teacher's table and then sitting down. Within minutes, however, they've turned to face the rest of the class and are making the most of their vantage point by using it to carry on conversations with the rest of the group and to generally show off. The teacher is now trying to do a question-and-answer session with the learners. She doesn't appear to know anyone's name. Instead, when she's asked a question she points and says, 'You!' But she doesn't really get any answers, apart from, 'How should I know?' and 'Pass'.

By this time you're feeling really quite depressed, so you leave the room and close the door quietly behind you.

We're going to look in a minute at how a different teacher might handle this situation; but first you may find it useful to make a note of what you yourself would have done if confronted with this class. Before we visit the class again, let's just remind ourselves of the theory behind the idea that the Relationship between teacher and learners can have a crucial impact on motivation.

Relationship and Reward

Some psychologists argue that it's possible to locate and nurture the sense of intrinsic motivation in all learners, and as teachers in FE that's an idea we definitely need to explore. Carl Rogers, for example, suggested that the best way to achieve this is by building a positive relationship between teacher and learner (Rogers, 1983). One of Rogers' famous phrases, which you may well have heard already, is **unconditional positive regard**. What he meant by this is that if the teacher is able to build up a relationship of mutual trust with the learner and demonstrate an unconditional acceptance of the learner just as he or she is, the learner will feel sufficiently safe and valued to begin to develop his or her full potential, not only as a learner, but also as a balanced and fulfilled human being. This, then, is the connection between Relationship and Reward: that in creating a positive relationship with the learners, a teacher enables them to discover that learning and personal development can be rewarding for their own sake. However, argued Rogers, this process also requires teachers to be honestly and authentically themselves and not to hide behind the role or mask of The Teacher.

Now, you might well, in your more cynical moments, find these two ideas – of being totally honest and at the same time demonstrating unconditional positive regard for your learners (at least the ones like those in the class we've just witnessed) – mutually incompatible, if not downright ludicrous. But don't worry, because we'll be seeing in a minute how a teacher might adopt a pragmatic approach to that scenario. First, let's just take note of another set of ideas that connect Relationship with Reward. Abraham Maslow – he of the famous **Hierarchy of Needs** – suggests, like Rogers, that all learners have the innate capacity to feel motivated towards achieving their highest potential, but that they can't access this until a whole set of other needs have been met (Maslow, 2013). They need to feel physically safe, for example, and free from pain. They also need to feel accepted and valued. This ties in well with our discussions in Chapter 1 about the range of demotivating factors that can lie behind a learner's reluctance to engage. And this is also where Maslow's and Rogers' ideas can, from the practical point of view of the FE teacher, be said to converge: the teacher's relationship with the learner provides the opportunity for building both a sense of safety and a sense of being valued. We refer to Rogers and Maslow as humanists. They are both proponents of the belief that every human being has the potential to become self-motivated. As teachers, then, we should be able to tap into this and use the way we relate to our learners to unlock that potential in them.

Using the way we relate to motivate our learners

So let's see now how that might work if we take the class that we met earlier on in this chapter and give it to another teacher. His name is Davit Deera. If you ask him about 'unconditional positive regard' he'll come right back at you with one of his favourite sayings, which goes back way further than Carl Rogers. It is from Roger Ascham's *The Schoolmaster* (1570), and it goes: 'Sooner allured by love, than driven by beating, to attain good learning'. So never let anyone persuade you that motivating learners by making them feel valued is a soft, New Age kind of idea. It's at least four-and-a-half centuries old.

Davit arrives at the room before the learners. He makes sure the tables are arranged in a square with the learners' chairs arranged around three sides, and his on the fourth. As the learners start to arrive he welcomes each one by name as they come in. He speaks pleasantly to everyone, reminding them that this is the day their assignments are due in. By the time everyone is present he's checked with them all individually and discovered that no one has brought an assignment to hand in. He sits on his table facing the class and says, loudly enough to get their attention: 'Good to see you, everybody. Everybody all right?' He looks cheerfully around the three sides of the square, making clear eye-contact with everyone. He gets a few half-hearted responses and one or two cheeky smiles. 'Josh, you all right? Emily? Raz? You okay? Okay. Well look, I'm a bit worried about you lot. Tell me why I'm a bit worried.' He gets a number of responses, not many of them sensible or even polite; but he homes in on the one he wants, ignoring the rest. 'Dead right. Raz is dead right. I'm worried about you because none of you – not one of you – has remembered to bring your assignment in. So I need to hear from you why that is, because you know what? I'm really disappointed. Why do you think I'm disappointed? Sunjeev, why do you think I'm disappointed?'

'Because you think we're a bunch of losers,' says Sunjeev, and gets a laugh.

'Wrong. And it's not often you get a question wrong, Sunjeev.' This also gets a laugh. 'You are not losers. No way. I'll tell you what you are, though . . . ' And here he gets a lot of laughter and rude comments. 'What you lot are is my all-time favourite group.'

Among the good-natured scoffing and jeering a learner can be heard saying mockingly, 'Aaaah, bless!'

'So what I want us to do,' says Davit, 'is have a bit of a heart-to-heart about what's happening here. I'm here to help you. I want to see you guys succeed like you deserve to. So tell me why there are no assignments ready today. What's the problem?'

He gets a number of facetious answers, most of them from the two noisiest lads. But then, as he continues to listen, nodding but not otherwise responding, he begins to get a few serious answers. Emily asks what's the point of handing assignments in when you never get them marked and you never get them back. Raz says he wasn't aware today was the deadline, and several others agree that this was never made clear. Josh says he couldn't understand what he was supposed to be doing in the assignment, and there's a lot of noisy support for this point. Someone else says the assignment was boring. 'Yeah,' say several others. 'It was. It was well boring.'

'Okay,' says Davit, 'thanks. Now we're getting somewhere. Let me just ask you one more thing. What do you think was the reason why you didn't know what to do and you didn't know when to hand it in? Did nobody go through this with you?'

There's no agreement on this one. After some further discussion, the learners seem prepared to concede that they were probably told but that they weren't listening. 'Well, then,' says Davit, 'let's see if we can cut a deal. If I promise to explain to you exactly what you need to do in this assignment so that you're all confident that you know what you're supposed to be doing, and if I promise to have the assignments marked and back to you within a week, and if we agree together a new hand-in date – okay? – will you all promise to do your best to get your assignments done and in for that new deadline?'

There are some reluctant nods and murmurs of assent. 'So is it a deal?' says Davit.

This time the response is a little bit more positive. Several people say, 'Deal', or 'Yeah'. They're all at least listening, and there's a general air of agreement and cooperation.

Then a voice pipes up: 'I don't see why you're making us do assignments. They're just boring, innit.'

Now, you may feel that was all too good to be true, or you may even suspect Davit was wasting his time. Will the group keep their side of the bargain and meet the new deadline they've negotiated? We may find that out in a later chapter. And clearly there was at least one dissenter not won over by Davit's approach. Nevertheless, there was a very clear difference between the ways in which the two teachers were conducting their relationship with those learners. We can set out the main characteristics of the two approaches as in the table on the next page to make a comparison between them.

Question

Earlier in this chapter you were asked to make a list of things about the first teacher's approach that you'd want to change. You might like to reflect now on how closely that list coincides with the left-hand column in the table on the next page.

Using Davit's approach as a starting point, we could draw up the following set of rules and call them:

Rules for building your Relationship with learners:

1   Interact with learners as individuals, not always as a crowd.

2   Learn their names and use them.

3   Engage in dialogue with the learners (this means listening to them as well as them listening to you).

What the first teacher does	What Davit does
She opens the lesson by shouting at learners to be quiet.	He begins the lesson by greeting each learner and welcoming them.
She treats learners as a group.	He treats learners as individuals.
She blames the class collectively for not handing in the assignment.	He speaks individually with each one in tacit acknowledgement that each might have different reasons for not completing the assignment.
She either doesn't know their names or sees no reason to use them.	He knows their names and uses them at every opportunity.
She consistently blames them.	He makes an opportunity to praise them.
She presents the non-submission of the assignment as a behaviour problem and an indication that these learners aren't worth bothering with.	He presents their failure to complete the assignment as a practical problem that he and they need to investigate together.
She uses existing classroom seating arrangements as an opportunity to punish or humiliate learners.	He organises a seating arrangement that encourages communication, cooperation and an equal valuing of each individual.
She sticks to her own agenda, so therefore attempts to carry on with a lesson despite the obvious lack of motivation.	He chooses on this occasion to respond to the learners' immediate needs by initiating a discussion to discover how the learners might be helped to regain their motivation.
She responds to their lack of motivation by asking questions about what they know.	He responds to their lack of motivation by asking questions about how they feel.
She demands that they listen to her.	He listens to them.
She orders the learners about.	He negotiates.
She judges and blames the learners.	He doesn't respond judgementally.
She makes it clear she doesn't like them or enjoy teaching them.	He makes it clear that he likes them and cares about them.
She's a poor role model because she doesn't appear motivated or enthusiastic about teaching them, but blames them for lack of motivation ('do as I say').	He's a good role model because he appears motivated and enthusiastic ('do as I do').

4   Use negotiation whenever appropriate.

5   Act as a role model for the positive interpersonal skills you'd like to see the learners display.

6   Convince the learners that you like them and care about them.

Some of these are quite a tall order to implement and sustain, particularly the last two, which can call for all your reserves of forbearing and self-control. All six are longer-term strategies than some of the reward tactics that we looked at in the previous chapter. This is inevitable because here we're dealing with the ways we relate, and relationships take time to build and consolidate. The initiative and the perseverance have to come from the teacher, and you may have to be prepared at first to feel as though it's going nowhere. But one of the key things to bear in mind with this approach is the seventh – and perhaps most important – rule of thumb, which is:

7 Avoid taking learner attitudes personally.

This can be very difficult to do, particularly if learners' abusive comments or excuses for not working are phrased as an attack against you. For example, they might tell you that your lesson, or the subject, or even you yourself are 'BORING'. 'Boring' is often the catch-all criticism made by 14–19-year-old learners. It may be literally true that you or your lessons are boring, in which case you'll find some help in identifying whether this is so, and if so how to address it, in Chapter 5. What's much more likely, however, is that the learners find themselves unable to engage with the lesson for one of the reasons we explored in Chapter 1, and they express this inability or unwillingness to engage as 'boredom'. If you take learners' lack of motivation as a personal affront, as the first teacher in this chapter seemed to do, your resentment and sense of personal injury will form an obstacle to any sound relationship that you could have built with the learners. As the teacher you are a target for all their resentments arising from their past experiences of being taught. If you can just take that on the chin, retain your cool, be yourself and continue to reassure them that you feel no corresponding negativity towards them, the learners will almost always begin to see you eventually as the teacher as 'helper' rather than the teacher as 'oppressor'. But this can take an enormous effort of will and perseverance.

However, you can also get some encouraging results in the short term, as we saw from Davit's interaction with the class. Trust takes time to build; but an open manner, a positive approach and a tactical use of people skills can achieve immediate results.

'Unconditional positive regard'

I promised earlier that we could take a pragmatic approach to this one, and so it might be useful just to unpack Rule 6 a little further. Rule 6 states:

6   Convince the learners that you like them and care about them.

And indeed we can see Davit working at that when he tells the group:

'What you are is my all-time favourite group.'

This may quite possibly be far from the truth. How could we know? But in a way, that's beside the point. From a practical point of view you may not always feel an 'unconditional positive regard' for all your learners, *but you can behave as though you do*. I'm sure this advice would have Rogers, who placed so much emphasis on authenticity, spinning in his grave. But we're talking here about busy FE teachers, not psychologists, and we have to make best use of the tools at hand. If you behave in a way that demonstrates a positive regard for your learners, you will also be modelling for them the sort of attitudes and behaviours that you would like to see them develop in themselves. It's a case of keeping your natural irritations or frustrations out of the equation as far as you possibly can.

A useful way of reinforcing the idea that you have a positive regard for all your learners is to acknowledge that the group is a collection of individuals and not some featureless collective. Davit's strategy of treating the learners as individuals goes deeper than an operational use of, say, differentiation or individual learning plans. It's about how he relates to them. It's also a flexible, longer-term strategy. For example, he chooses to sacrifice a substantial part of the session for discussing their problems with the assignment, rather than sticking to his lesson plan. This is because, in the long run, this should prove the more productive option in terms of getting them to complete and submit their work.

Combating bullying

Davit encountered a lot of problems with this group, but bullying wasn't one of them. However, one of the most demotivating experiences for a learner is being bullied. It epitomises that Big Demotivator, Fear, and a chapter about building motivation on a willingness to relate is a good place to look at how we can combat this most negative of relationships. Bullying presents us, as teachers, with a double problem: how to address the bullying behaviour, and how to support and motivate the learner who has been on the receiving end.

Some strategies teachers find useful include:

- Careful observation of group dynamics. Victims of bullies are often afraid to come forward, so don't assume that not being told about it means it's not happening.

- Drawing attention regularly to the college's anti-bullying policy and the consequences of bullying behaviour. This may sound obvious, but it can be done in a routine way without being directed at anyone in particular, and can provide a victim with the reassurance and confidence to come forward.

- Being approachable. No learner is going to tell you he or she is in trouble if you're just as scary as the bully.

- If you suspect bullying is going on, raise the topic in class without naming names, and negotiate an agreed code of conduct. This is a way of harnessing peer pressure. If the majority of learners – those not involved – feel some ownership of the agreed code, they'll help you 'police' it.

- If you suspect bullying is going on, target the ringleaders and use all the tactics at your disposal to keep them on task. This is a way of creating opportunities for them to receive attention for positive reasons, helping them redefine themselves as winners for the RIGHT reasons and not just because they can intimidate someone else. Also, the knowledge that they are under scrutiny should provide an obstacle to bullying behaviour.

- If you detect a clear case of bullying, challenge it directly and follow college disciplinary procedures to the letter. The most effective way to motivate victims to come forward is to demonstrate – on an institutional level – that bullying will not be tolerated. This is most important because, sadly, the obverse is also true: that the most effective way to encourage bullies is to demonstrate that the college's anti-bullying policy doesn't work.

High expectations and self-fulfilling prophecies

Finally, a word about praise. We can link this to Davit's use of unconditional positive regard. If learners can be made to feel valued, they can also be made to feel capable of attaining realistic goals. 'You can all do this if you try' is a far better motivator than 'Anybody who can't do this shouldn't be here.' The most effective tactics here are to:

- Always describe goals as achievable ('*When* you've done this' rather than '*If* you get this done').

- Praise individuals but not at the expense of the rest of the group (not 'Well done! You're the only one who. . .' but 'Well done! And well done, everybody. . .').

- Keep telling them what a good group they are (Davit uses this tactic quite unashamedly).

- Tell them you're looking forward to reading their work, when you're getting them to hand it in – and make sure you look enthusiastic.

- Find something to praise or admire. There's almost always something, even if it's only the colour of their ring-binder. The idea is to make them think of themselves as winners in some context, however small.

Summary

In this chapter we've explored the importance of the teacher's relationship with the learners as a motivating factor. We've come up with a set of seven rules and conceded that they may require medium to long-term implementation before their full effectiveness becomes apparent. They may also call for considerable self-control on the part of the teacher. But whoever claimed that teaching in FE was easy? The rules are:

1 Interact with learners as individuals, not always as a crowd.

2 Learn their names and use them.

3 Engage in dialogue with the learners (this means listening to them as well as them listening to you).

4 Use negotiation whenever appropriate.

5 Act as a role model for the positive interpersonal skills you'd like to see the learners display.

6 Convince the learners that you like them and care about them.

7 Avoid taking learner attitudes personally

This chapter has also explained why it is wise in terms of learner motivation for FE teachers to:

- Be vigilant for cases of bullying.
- Remember that high expectations can be a self-fulfilling prophecy.

4 Encouraging motivation through Respect for self, for others and for Rules

In the previous chapter we talked a little about respect in terms of how we, as teachers, can model good practice for our learners by treating them with the sort of respect that we'd expect them to show for others. In this chapter we're looking at respect again but in the wider sense – Respect with a capital R. It's what we refer to when we talk about trying to encourage a 'Culture of Respect'. In this context we understand Respect to encompass a range of meanings, which include appropriate behaviour and attitudes, compliance with rules, consideration for others, and so on. Some FE colleges – and perhaps this includes your own – have adopted their own 'Respect policy', which sets out for learners the parameters of acceptable behaviour. The rules are often of a practical kind – and hopefully not so numerous as to be difficult to keep in mind – dealing with use of mobile phones or unacceptable language, and issues of a similar nature. They are designed to create and maintain an environment in which learners feel motivated to learn, unhindered by distractions or the disruptive behaviour of others. In FE, therefore, these two concepts – Respect and Rules – are increasingly interrelated, and in this chapter we'll be considering ways in which both of these can provide us with strategies for motivating our learners.

Authority and Power

One of the themes of this chapter will be that, in terms of motivating FE learners, *Authority* is more appropriate than Power, and *Respect* is more effective than Fear. To see exactly what we mean by that, let's define those terms a little further. Power is something most FE teachers would agree they don't have much of. As teachers we may have very little say over which learners are recruited to our classes, or whether they are allowed to remain. We can also certainly feel very powerless when it comes to imposing sanctions for behaviour that we find unacceptable, as we discussed in Chapter 2. Authority, on the other hand, is something we may very well lay claim to. Our authority may arise from our depth of subject knowledge or skills, our confidence in our professional practice, or our ability to create order and a sense of purpose in our classroom or workshop. For example, Sly Cunningham, whom we met in Chapter 2, probably has no real power in his college. He can't 'hire or fire' learners or enforce any serious sanctions; but it is clear, as we see him handle the group of learners, that he is able to establish a certain authority in a way that the teacher who was there before him could not. The same is true of Davit, whom we met in Chapter 3. Some might accuse him of having quite a 'soft' approach; but he nevertheless is able to exert authority to the extent that he gets learners listening and negotiating and entering into a dialogue with him. That sort of authority is essential to building a culture of respect, which will serve as a motivating factor for our learners.

Respect and Fear

Now let's look at Fear and Respect. Fear, as we saw in Chapter 1, is one of the Four Big Demotivators. We don't want to instil fear into our learners because, in the context of motivation to learn, it's generally seen to be counter-productive (think of Maslow's Hierarchy of Needs, which we mentioned in the last chapter). It wasn't always seen this way, of course; and in some contexts a 'healthy fear' is still used to encourage a disciplined and accurate response to training – in the armed services, for example. However, thankfully, inspiring fear is no longer a respectable part of the teacher's repertoire. Inspiring Respect, on the other hand, is a different matter.

The reason we're pairing those two together – fear and respect – is because there's an area of overlap that we might refer to as 'keeping people on their toes'. If we respect someone, it usually means that we want to win their approval. This is why winning learners' respect can be a vital precursor to getting them motivated. Scaring them, on the other hand, is likely to have just the opposite effect. So how do we differentiate between these two ways of keeping people on their toes? How do we make sure we don't cross the line between winning respect and resorting to fear tactics?

Motivating through Respect versus motivating by Fear

Winning Respect	Fear tactic
1. Maintain self-control, even under provocation. This doesn't mean you don't respond to provocative behaviour, but that your response should be measured and tactical – a response, not a knee-jerk reaction.	1. React to provocation with loss of temper. We saw a teacher do this in the last chapter. You'll probably remember that there was nothing in that outburst to win respect, and it was certainly scary.
2. Be consistent in applying rules. If you have rules, stick to them and make sure they apply to everyone equally – including yourself where appropriate (e.g. avoiding offensive language).	2. Apply rules unpredictably, unevenly and unfairly. Tolerate things one day that you won't tolerate on another, depending on your mood at the time. Unpredictability creates fear.
3. Be consistent in applying rewards and sanctions.	3. Apply rewards and sanctions on your own whim.
4. Be firm, but treat everyone equally and fairly.	4. Treat some learners with favouritism and others as targets to be regularly picked on.
5. Give accurate assessment feedback that indicates clearly to the learner what he or she needs to do in order to improve performance.	5. Give accurate assessment feedback that focuses only on what the learner has done wrong – and make the list as long as you can.
6. Use praise whenever there's an opportunity to do so.	6. Use criticism whenever it's possible to do so.
7. If you make promises, be seen to keep them.	7. Issue threats and dire warnings about the future.
8. Use your approval as a Reward.	8. Never show approval.
9. Use your disapproval as a withholding of Reward, so that learners are motivated by the desire to win your approval back.	9. Use your anger as a punishment, so that learners are 'motivated' by the need to placate your anger.
10. Learners feel motivated in the longer term because they like and respect you.	10. Learners are coerced short term into activity because they fear you.

Those are just ten ways in which we might define the difference between inspiring Respect and instilling Fear. You can probably add more of your own. Just as Sly and Davit, in previous chapters, demonstrate the positive use of Authority, they also present us with useful role models in terms of the way they go about earning the Respect of their learners. This is because Authority and Respect go together. Establish your Authority and you gain Respect. This is the positive approach to motivating learners, and likely to pay off in the longer term as well as having an immediate effect. It is of far more practical use to you than trying to wield a power you don't really possess in order to frighten learners into working. Fear may work in the short term, but in the long term it will only serve to reinforce learners' dislike of learning. Our first rule for this chapter, then, sets out the self-perpetuating behaviour cycle for motivational teaching:

Build authority through gaining learners' respect, and their respect through establishing your authority.

The no-nonsense approach

We're going to consider now how all this might look in practice. We've given Sly and Davit an honourable mention in this chapter. Now let's look at a teacher who bases her entire approach to motivation on establishing a culture of respect in her classes, and above all a regime of respect for the teacher. Her name is Amy Harman, and let's say she is successful at motivating groups of learners whom many of her colleagues despair of ever getting any work out of at all. As you watch her in action, see if you can identify which of the Respect strategies (listed in the table above) she is using, and with what degree of success. You might also like to look out for her use of other strategies that we've discussed in earlier chapters, such as Reward.

The lesson

The learners – a group of 17–18-year-olds on a Level 2 programme – are having a workshop session to complete their assignment. They are seated in five small groups, each around a separate table. Most have nothing in front of them – no paper or tablet or folder or laptop or pen – and their body language, in most cases, seems to suggest that they are exhausted, debilitated or depressed. The only person in the room who is exhibiting any energy at this moment is the teacher, Amy Harman. So how is she going to get them working?

> Amy: Well, look. They're here, aren't they? If they're sufficiently motivated to turn up, then I'm in with a chance. I have something to build on. So the first thing I'm going to try is to remind them of our agreement. As soon as everybody at a table has completed their assignment to my satisfaction, that table gets to leave for an early break. Let's see what happens.

What happens is that the learners at four of the five tables start getting out their work and, with a lot of sighing and huffing and puffing, begin to check with one another on their progress so far. At the fifth table, however, there's a mutiny going on. Jaz and Ben are refusing to do any work. 'Like what would I want to do it for, anyway, innit?' demands Jaz. Laura and Lois, at the same table, ignore the boys and begin working together. Amy, meanwhile, strides about between the tables, looking over shoulders and giving encouragement. For the moment she is ignoring Jaz and Ben. But is that a good idea?

> Amy: Yes, it is. I've just got all the rest to start working. If I now concentrate all my attention on the two who aren't working, then I've lost the crucial moment and I'll probably not be able to jump-start them all again. So I'm just reinforcing and encouraging the others, and once I'm satisfied they're ticking along nicely I'll see what I can do about Jaz and Ben. They're grumbling and refusing to work, but they're not disrupting anybody else's learning at the moment.

While Amy is giving some help and advice to the group on the far side of the room, there's a bit of a clatter of chairs scraping, and she turns to see Laura and Lois carrying their work over to join their friends at an all-girl table, leaving Jaz and Ben the fifth table to themselves. Amy walks over and asks the two girls sternly what it is they're doing. The girls say they don't want to share a table with Jaz and Ben; they want to work with a table that's got a chance of finishing early. 'Okay, Lois and Laura,' says Amy, conversationally, but making sure the whole class can hear her. 'I think that's a good idea. I'm happy for you to move. You're working hard and you deserve an opportunity to try for an early break. So settle down quickly and you can carry on.'

Why does Amy give in so easily?

> Amy: But this was an absolute gift! It allowed me to underline the 'work hard – finish early' rule, and to reinforce the fact that Jaz and Ben's non-cooperation doesn't

serve their own best interests. It also gave me an opportunity to reinforce the fact that I'm the boss. I made sure everyone had no doubt that the move went ahead because I allowed it. And of course I took the opportunity to walk over and speak to the girls directly rather than shouting to them across the whole class, because the last thing I want is a reputation as a Shouter. In my experience, Shouters rarely win respect. And I can't expect the learners to keep the noise down if I'm setting the example of shouting, can I?

Very soon, however, Jaz and Ben are certainly failing to 'keep the noise down'. They are calling across to one of the other groups, trying to get a discussion going about where everybody's going on Friday night. Ben has also begun to do acrobatics with his chair, tipping backwards on it until it's precariously balanced with the front legs well off the floor. Amy turns suddenly from the group she's been working with, and walks quickly and purposefully right up to Ben and says firmly, but not loudly, 'You're breaking Health and Safety regulations, Ben. Bring that chair and come over here with me. I want your help with something.' Without waiting for a reply, she turns and walks back to the group she was working with. Ben, grinning, follows, dragging his chair and making as much noise with it as possible. 'I need you to do some proofreading for this group,' says Amy. 'You're a good speller. Help them with the proofreading so they can finish and have an early break. You help them do that and you can go with them. Do we have a deal?' Actually, it seems they do. Ben sits down and, with a lot of grinning and preening, says, 'Give it here, then,' and begins reading through some of the group's work. But wasn't this a bit of a high-risk tactic on Amy's part?

Amy: *Well, yes. But the best tactics are often risky, and it paid off, didn't it? And in actual fact it was probably less risky than it seemed. I didn't shout at him or order him about in front of the whole class, so I wasn't risking a public confrontation or a highly visible show of non-compliance on his part. I stated clearly which rule he was breaking, so that my intervention couldn't be construed as simply me being intolerant or irritable at the fact he wasn't working. I told him what I wanted him to do and gave him no time to think about it, no time to think up a smart reply. I turned immediately away. And that was a bit of play-acting, a way of suggesting to him – and all the rest who were watching – that it would never even cross my mind that he might not comply. It's saying, 'I'm not the sort of teacher you mess with.' And as far as Ben's concerned it's also saying to him, 'I think you're a reasonable bloke who'll be willing to give me a bit of help.' Plus it's a way of making him feel valued.*

But didn't he just end up getting rewarded for his messing about?

Amy: Look, I found something to praise him for – his spelling – instead of reinforcing his 'I'm a waster' act by giving him a bollocking for messing about. In terms of respect, no one's going to say it's unfair that he got my attention for being a good speller. I made a deal with them that there's a pay-off for getting their work done. And hey, I got him working, didn't I?

The same can't be said, however, for Jaz. He's still making a lot of noise and trying to get loud exchanges going with the other four tables, making personal comments that are becoming increasingly offensive. Amy goes and sits at the table with him. 'What?' he says belligerently. And when she doesn't answer immediately, he raises his voice: 'What?'

'Jaz,' she says calmly, 'why are you here?'
'I don't f***ing know, do I? How should I know?'
'Do you want me to help you get started on your assignment?'
'No, thanks.' And then, when she continues looking at him, he asks again, aggressively: 'What?'

At this point one of the other groups calls across to Amy that they've finished and can they go. She gets up and goes over to check their work. They're already putting their coats on. Satisfied, she says, 'Well done', and tells them they can leave. As they're leaving, Jaz gets up, picks up his sports bag and heads for the door. The three remaining groups set up a complaint that this isn't fair. He hasn't done any work. He shouldn't be able to leave. Amy follows him to the door and when they are just outside it she reminds him calmly that he'll fail the module if his assignment isn't handed in to her by the end of the day. Back inside the classroom she says to the others, 'Okay, now listen up. You all played by the rules and you've put the work in and it looks as though you're going to pass the module. Jaz didn't want to play by the rules and at the moment it looks like he's going to fail it. What's unfair about that?' This seems to satisfy them. They finish off the work and leave. Everyone gets an early break, including Amy. But the fact remains, she failed with Jaz.

Amy: Okay, yes, I failed. I didn't find a way to get him motivated. But I did a pretty good job of not allowing him to undermine the motivation of the others. And sometimes that's the best you can expect.

Do you agree? Amy's strategy seems to be:

If you can't find a way to motivate the learner, find a way to prevent him or her undermining the motivation of the rest.

She did this in a series of steps:

1   She gave her attention initially to the learners she'd succeeded in motivating, in order to establish them securely in working mode.

2   She isolated Jaz by turning her attention to Ben and drawing him into a motivated group.

3   When Jaz's lack of motivation threatened to seriously disrupt the motivation of others, she interrupted his disruptiveness by sitting next to him.

4   When he got up to leave she avoided the potential head-on confrontation, which would have disrupted everyone else's learning.

5   Although Jaz's getting away with it could have undermined the morale of those who'd actually stuck to the deal and worked, Amy presents what has happened in such a way that Jaz is seen as the loser and those who've done the work as winners.

Through every stage she makes sure she is seen to be firm but fair. Jaz is reminded of the consequences of not doing his assignment; those who do the assignment are rewarded as promised; she doesn't lose her temper or make vain threats; she creates an environment in which those who want to work can, and those who set out to disrupt that work encounter consequences of one kind or another.

You may argue that she was lucky; that her approach couldn't have worked so well if she'd been dealing with a class where the majority of learners were just like Jaz. And you may be right. You could also argue that her no-nonsense approach made no allowance for the possibility that Jaz may have been struggling with personal or health problems that left him demotivated and irritable. That's because Amy is just a two-dimensional teacher. She's here to represent the Respect approach. Davit, similarly two-dimensional with his unconditional positive regard, might have concentrated on asking Jaz how he was feeling. The point here is that:

When it comes to motivating learners, for maximum effectiveness we need to feel confident about using more than one approach.

Motivation in non-standard classrooms and beyond

Respect for rules can be a major Health and Safety requirement in some teaching environments; this strategy then becomes essential. In workshops and labs, and particularly at off-site visits, there may be extra distractions, more opportunities for covert off-task activities, or even – and here's the ultimate in disengaged behaviour – opportunities for absconding altogether. In non-standard classrooms with fixed furniture, such as IT rooms or labs, there are the added complications of lack of flexibility about seating and grouping, which may make it difficult to establish or maintain eye-contact with learners. In such environments the keys to motivation are:

- a firm emphasis on the practical work for which the environment is designed

- a careful explanation of the Health and Safety rules, including how and why they are applied

- clear schedules and deadlines (and head-counts where learning takes place off-site).

Modelling politeness

Respect, politeness and appropriate behaviour are not innate qualities. We can't expect learners to demonstrate any of these unless they have seen them in operation. This is why it's essential that our own behaviour is – as far as possible – a model that we would wish our learners to follow. We can't make demands of learners – for example, to be enthusiastic, polite, hardworking and committed – that we aren't able to meet ourselves. Current government advice that teachers should model polite behaviour may have had a rocky ride in the press, but it's based on sound motivational principles. After all, we don't expect our learners to be motivated and to show respect for us unless we've demonstrated our own motivation and our respect for them.

Summary

In this chapter we've looked at the importance of Respect in motivating learners. We've come up with some tactics for gaining the respect of our students. These are:

- Control your own behaviour first, and maintain self-control, even under provocation.
- Model the respectful language, attitude and behaviour you wish the learners to adopt.
- Apply rules consistently...
- ... but don't have so many of them that they can't all be kept in mind!
- Clearly explain the consequences of breaking rules.
- Clearly explain which rule has been broken.
- Be consistent with rewards and sanctions.
- Be seen to be firm but fair.
- Be seen to keep promises.
- Wherever possible, motivate with praise rather than criticism.
- Win over the disruptive ringleader, or discredit them. (Amy employs both these tactics, winning over Ben and discrediting Jaz.)
- As with the other Big Motivators, don't rely on Respect and Rules alone. For maximum effectiveness you'll need to draw on other strategies as appropriate.
- Respect for rules can be essential to Health and Safety in some teaching environments.

We've also taken the pragmatic view that you can't win them all, and that in some situations you may have to settle for the fall-back position, which is:

If you can't find a way to motivate the learner, find a way to prevent him or her undermining the motivation of the rest.

Above all, we need to remember that Respect works both ways. Learners will not respect the teacher if the teacher doesn't show respect for them.

5 Waking learners up with some Razzmatazz: putting the entertainment value into learning

Not for everyone, you may think. But don't mistake what we're about here. This approach shouldn't have you strapping on your tap shoes or practising new jokes. Entertaining learners is not the same thing as teaching them or supporting their learning. There's no particular merit in keeping a class happy and laughing for forty minutes if at the end of it they've achieved none of the required outcomes and learned nothing relevant to the aims of their course. But if you can keep them happy and laughing for forty minutes *and in the process support them in achieving their learning objectives*, then you'll have won a double success. They'll have learned the prescribed lesson content and they'll also have learned something arguably even more important, which is that learning in itself can be enjoyable.

Enjoyment as antidote

Of course, 'happy and laughing for forty minutes' may be a bit of a big ask; some days you'd no doubt be pleased to settle for five minutes of mild amusement. But the principle we're looking at here is an important one. What it amounts to is this: learners will be motivated if they find learning enjoyable. This sounds almost too obvious to be worth stating. But think for a moment about those Four Big Demotivators we discussed in Chapter 1, and consider how a realisation that learning can be interesting or fun could act as an antidote to those.

Demotivator	How the antidote works
Fear The learner fears that their lack of skill or knowledge will be exposed, or that he or she will be subjected to ridicule or anger from the teacher or other learners.	A learning activity that is fun can draw in the frightened learner because it usually carries no echoes of the punitive or threatening experiences that caused fear to build up.
Boredom The learner's previous experience of learning is that it's boring – either because it's too easy or too hard or is, in actual fact, really boring.	Rediscovering that learning can be fun provides the learner with an alternative point of reference. Differentiation within the activity allows the learner to engage at his or her own level.
Previous Negative Experience The learner's previous experience of learning is a negative or destructive one, perceiving the teacher as The Enemy.	Novel and innovative activities create an alternative model for the learner in which learning is a positive, enjoyable experience and the teacher is someone who provides this.
Loss of Hope Learners may feel there's no hope of succeeding with learning, or qualifying, or gaining employment.	New activities, providing accessible goals which are fun to achieve, make everyone feel like a winner, and provide a basis for hope.

A bit of what we're calling 'Razzmatazz' can create a new set of positive expectations in the learner which, in time, can come to supersede the old negative attitudes that sapped their motivation.

So here's a summary of what we've said so far:

- It is not enough simply to entertain learners. This is not the same thing as teaching them or supporting their learning.

- In the process of teaching the prescribed lesson content you have the opportunity to establish that learning in itself can be enjoyable.

- Learners will be motivated if they find learning fun.

- The use of imaginative teaching and learning methods is an effective way of combating the Four Big Demotivators.

What is Razzmatazz and how does it work?

Before we go any further, there are a number of points you might want to raise about this approach. These may include:

1   Don't we all do this anyway?

2   I've tried doing interesting stuff with them, but it doesn't work because they won't listen or cooperate. How do you get around that?

3 I'm a teacher, not an entertainer. This just isn't my style. Why should I bother?

4 Novel methods might work with some learners, but not necessarily with all of them. And it only takes one or two determinedly disengaged learners to spoil it for the rest. How do you get over that one?

5 Why should I go to a lot of trouble to plan interesting stuff when the learners just aren't bothered?

6 Isn't introducing 'fun' into lessons just a recipe for mayhem?

7 How do you introduce interesting activity or novelty into a timetable that's already pared down to the minimum? There just isn't time.

The most useful way to address these questions is by seeing how a proponent of this approach would answer them. Let's call her Loretta Starr, motivator extraordinaire. Here's what she has to say.

1. Don't we all do this anyway?

Well no, I don't think all of us do. And there are lots of reasons why that's so. One is that novel learning activities – like games or competitions or simulations – are also quite high risk in terms of classroom control. I don't just mean that they give more scope for learners to run riot or to sabotage the lesson by refusing to join in. I also mean they're difficult in terms of planning. How do we estimate the time they'll take, or what direction they'll go off in, or whether they'll trigger questions from learners that we can't answer? And this approach can be problematic in terms of resourcing, too. The room layout might appear unsuitable for anything but teacher activity and passive learning – I'm thinking here of an IT room or a lab. So there are all sorts of reasons why it might not occur or appeal to us to use this approach. And when you're pushed for time it's hard to be inventive. Then, of course, there'll be teachers who've tried to plan exciting stuff for their classes, but just got so demotivated by the lack of response that they don't bother any more. What I want to do here is to demonstrate that it's worth persevering, and to give some practical advice on how you can make it work.

For each of the objections people put up against using this approach, there's a perfectly good counter-argument; and I would suggest that the advantages far outweigh the disadvantages. Let's look a bit more closely at those objections and see how they stand up.

So my answer to the question, if I have to summarise, is: No, we don't all do this already. But we should, and almost certainly could.

Objection	Answer
It could get noisy and out of control.	Yes, it could. But are these particular unmotivated learners currently quiet and well-controlled? If not, you have nothing to lose and much to gain.
Learners might sabotage the lesson or activity by refusing to join in.	Indeed they might. But are they responding to the current approach and engaging with their learning? If not, you again have nothing to lose and much to gain.
It's impossible to incorporate innovative activities into the lesson plan because you can never estimate how much time they'll take.	If it looks as though the activity will overrun, that can only be good news, because it means the learners are feeling motivated enough to stick with it. You can always find or invent a shortcut to the end, or draw it to a close in time for a debrief with the promise of continuing next time. If it turns out to take no time at all – because it was too easy or learners don't engage with it – have Plan B up your sleeve.
Something unpredictable might happen.	Good.
It may raise questions from learners that we can't answer.	If learners are asking questions at all, take it as a sign they're motivated and count it a success. If they ask questions you can't answer, say so, and take the opportunity to offer a prize to anyone who can find the answer by next lesson.
The room layout might appear unsuitable for anything but a formal, teacher-centred approach.	That's no excuse, unless you're trying to organise musical chairs or ballroom dancing. There's always something you can do to inject a bit of novelty, whatever the seating arrangements. See the suggestions at the end of this chapter.

2. I've tried doing interesting stuff with them, but it doesn't work because they won't listen or cooperate. How do you get around that?

Sometimes what appears interesting to us as the teacher simply doesn't engage the learners' interest at all. We might spend a long time planning some quite elaborate activity, and then feel disheartened and rejected when we can't get the learners to engage with it. The trick is to start from where their interest lies – within reason, obviously! Sport is a good one, and music. And there are always key TV programmes that are the buzz at any one time. You need to watch and listen, and pick up on some of this so that you've got a few ideas to work with.

I think another answer to this is to be very clear about what it is you want them to do, break that down in your head into small, doable steps, and then find ways to motivate them at each step towards that goal. So let's say you've decided that what you want them to do is to cooperate and stay on task for the whole of the lesson.

That's too big. So what you do is say to yourself, 'I want them to be motivated for the first ten minutes, so we'll make the question and answer session at the beginning follow the format of *Pointless*. And then I want them to be motivated for the next ten minutes, so I'll present them with another activity – maybe based on voting ideas out, using the same voting procedure as on *Big Brother*', and so on. If I decide what I want is for them to get their work done and in on time, I take it in week by week. Again, the bite-size approach. I have two teams and we get a huge snakes and ladders game going on the screen and at the beginning of each lesson the teams go up a ladder for every task handed in, and down a snake every time one of their team misses a deadline. It sounds infantile, but in fact it works really well because it injects a bit of fun into the process as well as a bit of friendly rivalry, and it doesn't necessarily involve naming names. A bit of competition, if it's well handled, can work wonders. Look how much time they spend watching football or *X Factor*. The trick is to keep it non-threatening and make sure it doesn't expose anyone to failure or ridicule, because then it would just be counter-productive. You'd be back where you started.

You say they won't listen. Well, if a group's not good at listening, instigate listening games: identifying sounds or working out the next item in sequence – whatever best fits your subject area. If they're not good at cooperating, introduce activities where success requires cooperation, whether in a pair or a team or among the group as a whole; pool clues to solve some problem, for example. That's when you're really winning; when you're facilitating student activity that not only manages to engage the group, but also helps them develop the skills they need to move forward.

And the final thing I'd want to say in answering this question is: it's not enough for you to know exactly what it is you want the learners to do. You also have to communicate that clearly and effectively to the learners themselves. This means making sure you're heard. And because that's more easily said than done, I'll be talking a bit more about that in answer to a later question.

Key points

- When planning innovative activities, start from where the learners' interest lies.
- Be clear about what it is you want learners to do or achieve, and break that down into smaller steps.
- Competition can be an effective motivator, if you can ensure it remains friendly.
- Don't introduce activities that risk exposing anyone to failure or ridicule.
- When planning activities to engage the group, focus on developing those skills they need to move forward.

3. I'm a teacher, not an entertainer. This just isn't my style. Why should I bother?

You don't have to be a wild extrovert or a stand-up comic to try this strategy. Indeed, the most important aspect of this approach is, I think, in the planning. Success with this strategy involves the careful choice and design of activities to meet the needs of a specific group of learners. It calls not so much for performance skills as for creativity of thought. We all try to find ways to spark learners' interest. What this approach does, really, is to find ways to spark learners' interest *through the content and planning of our lessons*, rather than – say – through offering rewards, or imposing sanctions, or concentrating on learners' emotional needs. That's why I emphasise the planning stage as so crucial. As teachers, we're all involved in the planning as well as the implementation of our lessons. What I'm suggesting here is that we use dual starting points for our planning: don't just find ways to teach the required curriculum content, but find ways to teach it that will make your learners sit up and take notice. Literally! So I'd argue that this approach doesn't demand anything more from the teacher than is already implicit within their role.

Key points

- Find ways to spark learners' interest through the content and planning of your lessons.

- When planning, think not only about what has to be taught, but also about how it can be made to grab learners' interest.

---

4. Novel methods might work with some learners, but not necessarily with all of them. And it only takes one or two determinedly disengaged learners to spoil it for the rest. How do you get over that one?

Yes, motivating some learners is a real challenge. And that's a positive way to see it. It's a challenge and it's a problem to be solved. I've been talking here mainly about motivating groups, rather than individuals, because when we plan lessons it's usually for whole groups. But yes, often the lack of motivation comes down to a few individuals. You might get quite a number of learners engaged in learning activities, but there are always a few individuals who are much harder to win over, and they're the ones you have to really think about when you're planning your activities. What role are they going to play? How are you going to carry them along with you? This becomes even more important if the hardest ones to motivate are also the ringleaders. Because if you can win over the ringleaders and get them working, it's much easier to win over the rest. So how do I do it? Let me give some examples. And remember, there are two stages to this: the planning and the implementation.

Tactics for winning over the ringleaders

At the planning stage:

- Invent for them a key role in the activity, which a) makes them 'important'; while b) reducing their scope for disruption; and c) dislocating them slightly from the rest of the group (e.g. as judge or adjudicator, or as an observer who reports directly back to you).

- Make the activity one that draws on strengths you know the ringleaders possess (e.g. drawing, knowledge about martial arts, doing silly voices) so that they're more likely to join in (where they lead, the others may follow) and you'll have opportunities to praise them.

- If you're planning an interesting group activity, pre-plan the groups in such a way that your ringleaders are separated from the easily led and allocated to a group that will exert peer pressure on them to join in.

During the lesson:

- Find every opportunity to praise them, so that they don't need to turn to the other learners for validation.

- If this proves difficult, use the tactic of Positive Interpretation. This means choosing, wherever possible, to interpret examples of their behaviour in a positive way. For example, if they're refusing to answer a question, praise them for letting others have a go. If they're wandering about the room, praise them for offering to help other learners. Obviously, Positive Interpretation is not always possible nor indeed wise, for example if they're drinking tequila and playing with an air-rifle.

- Don't compete. Never go head to head with ringleaders. It's what they want, and it's your business to inspire them towards a more useful goal than this.

Having confrontations with ringleaders provides the learners with quite the wrong sort of entertainment.

- As far as possible, keep your sense of humour. Laugh with them (even if they're laughing at you).

- Do what you can to make ringleaders feel that a) you're not ruffled by them; and b) you actually quite like them (this may involve a lot of insincere smiling).

- If you begin to lose heart, always remember you're doing this for the sake of the rest of your learners – in order to prevent ringleaders from undermining their motivation even further.

Key points

- **If you can win over the ringleaders and get them working, it's much easier to motivate the rest.**
- **Employ Positive Interpretation by choosing, wherever possible, to interpret examples of ringleaders' disruptive behaviour in a positive way.**

5. Why should I go to a lot of trouble to plan interesting stuff when the learners just aren't bothered?

Because it may be that they just aren't bothered because you're *not* planning interesting stuff. Or perhaps you mean you're planning interesting stuff, but you can't get learners to engage with it. In which case have a look again at what I said in response to Question 2. The short answer is that, in almost every case, it pays off in the end to be imaginative and innovative. It wakes the learners up. It jolts them out of their expectations that this lesson is going to be 'boring' or is going to present a threat from which they have to retreat into disengagement.

And besides that, there's another pay-off to consider, and it's an important one. It's not only learners who get demotivated. As this question shows, it's teachers too. As you probably know from personal experience, looking for ways to inject novelty, impact and enjoyment into your lesson plans is an excellent way to re-energise your own commitment to teaching, and to remind yourself why you chose this profession in the first place. Even if the learner response is not always as wholehearted as you would hope, you nevertheless have the professional satisfaction of knowing you're taking positive action to get them to engage with the learning. In this way you break the vicious circle in which learners' lack of motivation causes you to lose your own, so that your teaching becomes tired and lacklustre and the learners grow even more disenchanted with it, and so on. Teacher enthusiasm can be half the battle. Why would learners get enthusiastic about the lesson if it's quite clear that the teacher isn't? And because you're the professional here, it's your responsibility to infect them with your enthusiasm, not their responsibility to motivate you with theirs.

Key points

- Imaginative and innovative learning activities can jolt the learners out of their expectations that the lesson is going to be 'boring' or somehow threatening.
- One of the most effective tactics you can use is a show of enthusiasm.

6. Isn't introducing 'fun' into lessons just a recipe for mayhem?

Sometimes. But fun is a good antidote to most negative expectations, and so usually worth the risk. If you want a fuller answer to this one, see my response to Question 1.

7. How do you introduce interesting activity or novelty into a timetable that's already pared down to the minimum? There just isn't time.

This is a good point, particularly in these difficult times when funding arrangements can tend to keep contact hours well down. Certainly the received wisdom is that teacher-centred learning – talking from the front, dictating notes, and so on – consumes less time than an approach where the emphasis is on learner activity. Let's be clear that I'm not arguing here that we abandon the teacher-led approach. It has its place and it's an important one. But it's only more effective in terms of time if the learners are actually learning from it. Many of our 14–19-year-old learners lack the skills required to take full advantage of this kind of teaching. For example, they may have no note-taking skills. The questions people risk omitting when arguing for the usefulness of the no-frills lecture, or the exposition, or the lengthy dictating of notes are: 'But are the learners learning?' and 'Are the objectives being achieved?' If the answer to that is 'No' or 'Not very effectively', then time is being wasted rather than gained.

It's worth considering, therefore, that there might be advantages in covering only some of the course objectives, but successfully, rather than covering all of them, but not very well. So when it comes to decisions about lesson content and time available the key criterion must not be **Will this method save time?** but **Will this method result in learners achieving the learning objectives?**

Key points

- 14–19-year-old learners may lack the skills required to respond to traditional teacher-centred methods.
- Traditional methods don't make effective use of time if they don't result in learners learning.

Summary

So that's Loretta's view. She's mentioned here some of the kinds of activities she finds useful in getting learners motivated. When adapting them for your own use they should be designed for their learning value as well as their entertainment value. Remember: entertaining is not the same thing as teaching. So you will need to be absolutely clear about the specified learning objectives – and make sure the learners are clear about them, too. Here are some of the activities mentioned in this chapter:

- games
- competitions
- quizzes
- challenges with prizes for the winner
- 'board' games
- activities linked to, or incorporating, learners' obvious interests, such as sport or music
- activities based on, or using elements of, popular TV programmes
- listening games (e.g. spot the subject-specific key words)
- cooperative team or pair games
- activities that draw on the strengths of the group or of individuals (e.g. motorbike maintenance, drawing, rapping).

You'll no doubt be able to build on this list by adding other ideas of your own. Finally, if you had to pick one piece of Loretta's advice as a guide for your future practice, it should be:

Always demonstrate enthusiasm. If you don't appear enthusiastic yourself, how can you expect enthusiasm from your learners?

6 Motivating individuals

The most effective teachers in FE will use some combination of the four approaches we've looked at in previous chapters. We've seen ways in which the four strategies – Reward, Relationship, Respect and Razzmatazz – can be effective; we've also seen their limitations. See examples below.

In Chapter 2, most of the class weigh in. . . telling Meena she ought to be able to wait 5 minutes. She gets very cross and storms out anyway.

In Chapter 3, Davit finds at least one learner has failed to respond to his relationship-building efforts:

A voice pipes up: 'I don't see why you're making us do assignments. They're just boring, innit.'

In Chapter 4, Amy's emphasis on respect works with everyone else but not with Jaz:

As they're leaving, Jaz gets up, picks up his sports bag and heads for the door. . . the fact remains, she failed with Jaz.

And even Loretta Starr admits that her approach of surprising learners out of their lethargy doesn't always work, saying:

There are always a few individuals who are much harder to win over.

One of the things we shall be doing in this chapter is showing how, when one approach appears not to work, we can try out others until we find one that does. One of the disadvantages our four caricature teachers have is that, although they may be experts in their particular motivational strategy, they'll inevitably encounter learners for whom that's not the most effective approach – as we've just seen. The real FE teacher needs to be able to use any or all of these tactics, and to judge with some accuracy what will work when and for which learner.

The defiant and uncooperative learner: motivating Meena

Let's take Meena first. None of the Rewards or Sanctions that Sly introduced for that class worked to deter Meena from making one of her regular 'toilet' trips out of the classroom to smoke a cigarette. She didn't respond to peer pressure, and the relative sense of order that Sly had established in the classroom didn't appear to have any impact on her own pattern of behaviour. If you had to think on your feet, as we have to when we're teaching, you'd probably conclude from this that as well as not responding to Reward, she probably won't be reached through Relationship either (she doesn't appear bothered what people think of her), nor through Respect (she's not responded in terms of motivation to a more orderly classroom). This leaves you with Razzmatazz. Perhaps Meena can be reached by presenting her with an activity so engaging that she'll forget all about leaving the room – at least for the next few minutes before the lesson ends. The time to present her with this, however, would not be at the point where she's making for the door. If she turns you down at this point, you've suffered a double setback, because she'll know what's on offer next time and it won't have its novelty impact. This requires you either to know about Meena's habit of walking out, or – if this class is new to you – to make a mental note and save your Razzmatazz for next time. The timing element is part of reflective teaching.

So what might you give Meena to do to keep her with the rest? If this is a pragmatic, thinking-on-your-feet decision, there's a range of high-profile, 'essential' activities you could recruit her to do. They include things like:

- Choose the winning group.

- Act as an observer and feed back to you.

- Look up a piece of vital information on the internet.

- Act as scribe and write group ideas on the flipchart, whiteboard or data projector.

If motivating Meena is an aim you defer until a subsequent lesson, you can incorporate it into your planning, choosing learning activities that provide opportunities for her to take a key (and potentially enjoyable) role, such as simulation or role play. Your thinking here would be: 'If she wants attention, let's provide it through a learning activity so that she doesn't have to seek it by making dramatic exits.' Too much trouble to go to for one learner? I don't think so. Meena's behaviour, and the way you respond to it, will have a big effect on the motivation of the rest of the group. You have four possible ways to address learner behaviour like Meena's:

1   Be seen to be letting her get away with it. This demotivates the rest.

2   Be seen to be responding ineffectively. This demotivates the rest.

3   Have a confrontation with her. This either entertains and distracts the rest, or scares them, but doesn't motivate them to learn.

4   Keep her engaged with the learning activities. Now she's no longer a distraction or source of demotivation for the others.

For those of you worrying that Meena has deep-seated problems, either physical or psychological, which cause her to keep leaving the room, please be reassured that she really is just going out for a cigarette! In the case of some learners, of course, there really are more serious and complicated factors at play and we'll be discussing these later in the chapter. For now, let's summarise what we've said so far:

- When you find one approach hasn't worked, make a professional judgement **based on what you've seen of the learner's behaviour** as to which approach might work better.

- **Choose your timing carefully**: a) don't force a confrontation; but b) don't lose the moment.

- Take this learner's characteristics into account **when planning** your next lesson.

- **Provide the opportunity** for the learner to gain attention or 'celebrity status' while engaged in learning, so he or she isn't driven to seek it through disengagement.

- **It's always worth it**, if only for the sake of keeping the other learners motivated.

So our key words here are: **observation, timing, planning, providing** and **JFDI (Just Frigging Do It!).**

The 'bored' learner

Just when Davit thought he'd established a good, positive working relationship with the class, up pipes this voice with the lament we hate to hear: 'But it's boring'.

This could undo all the hard work Davit has put into getting the rest of this group motivated. So what other strategy might be brought into play here? We don't know who this learner is, so we can't take an informed decision as we could with Meena. This time it's got to be trial and error. So let's see how our other teachers might employ their favourite strategies.

Sly's approach would offer two alternative tactics.

1. **Reward**. For example: 'But there's a prize for everyone who hands in an acceptable plan of their assignment at the end of this lesson.' Or 'But as soon as you've handed in an acceptable assignment plan you can go for an early break.'

2. **Withholding of Reward**. For example: 'That's fine. But it's a shame because if you don't get down to work on the assignment plan, you won't get an early break.' Or 'Oh dear. Because if you don't get some work done now, you'll have to miss the workshop session this afternoon and finish it then instead.'

Amy's approach, on the other hand, depending as it does on Respect for rules and acceptable codes of behaviour, might appear rather more confrontational. But she is too wise to be confrontational in front of an audience of learners, and so she would probably employ one of the following tactics:

- Engage the learner in a one-to-one conversation that was not overheard by the rest of the class, and point out firmly the consequences of non-completion.

- Take the learner's remark as an opportunity to draw up and agree a learning contract with the group, with rules to be adhered to on each side. Any further objections by individuals can then be referred to the group for adjudication.

- Avoid confronting it altogether by tactically ignoring the comment, and proceed as though she had never heard it. This tactic can work very well, as it avoids providing the individual with the time or platform to undermine the motivation of the rest of the learners. It has to be employed with care, however, because clearly there are some things it's unwise to ignore; you can't 'ignore' a comment or behaviour if it's obvious to everyone that you saw or heard it. Another obvious limitation of this tactic is that while it may succeed in sustaining the motivation of the rest of the group, it won't necessarily do much to motivate the individual in question.

And how could Loretta Starr's Razzmatazz be employed in this situation? Well, she'd certainly challenge that idea that the set task was inevitably going to be boring! Her response would probably be: 'Okay. Let's talk about how we can make this assignment more interesting for you.'

In other words, she would avoid getting into an argument along the lines of:

> Learner: Why should I do it? It's boring.
> Teacher: No, it's not boring.
> Learner: Yes it is. It's boring.
> Etc.

She believes that in order to be motivated the learner has to feel some interest in the task. If the learner expresses a lack of interest, Loretta is likely to take this at face value. She will have two tactics here, and will probably employ them both.

1 As an immediate response she will negotiate with the learner to find an idea or approach that will engage him or her. For example, the learner might become more interested in the task if it's adapted to involve interviewing other learners, or fact-finding on the internet, or inventing an imaginary organisation, or designing an ad for an ideal car, or writing from the point of view of a celebrity, and so on. Or she might propose a race against time, or against others, or teaming up or pairing up.

2 In her planning for subsequent lessons she will build in, wherever possible, the motivator that emerged from that negotiation. This is about responding to individual learning needs.

So, what we've said so far about motivating individual learners who claim to find the work boring is that you may have to try a number of approaches before finding the one that works. These can include:

- Reward or withhold Reward.

- Firmly point out the consequences of not doing the work.

- Draw up a learning contract, either with the group as a whole or with individual learners.

- Tactically ignore the comments about the task being 'boring' and hope they get on with it!

- Avoid getting into a 'No, it isn't' – 'Yes, it is' argument.

- Take the comment at face value and negotiate an approach or task that engages the learner's interest.

- Take that learner's individual learning needs (e.g. low boredom threshold) into account when planning subsequent lessons.

The learner who walks: getting Jaz motivated

You'll remember Jaz. He was the only learner in Chapter 4 whom Amy failed to get motivated. He was left isolated after she got his mate to join one of the working groups on the understanding that they could leave when the task was completed. Jaz, however, having tried and failed to disrupt the others, and having done no work himself, got up and left before the end of the lesson.

In an incident like this it's worth reflecting on what the key issues were, both for the teacher and for the individual learner. You might find it useful to go back for another quick look at Chapter 4 and do this for yourself. The points you come up with will probably include the following:

- Jaz hasn't responded positively to the No-Nonsense Respect approach. In fact it may even have antagonised him.

- He's a **demotivated demotivator**. This is a nice way of saying that he doesn't just sit there being 'bored' or refusing to work; he actively tries to undermine the motivation of the other learners, first by distracting them and then by making a nonsense of the 'work hard and leave early' deal.

- A situation that started out with a teacher attempting to motivate a learner (where success means that teacher wins and learner wins) changes into one where they are in direct conflict (success for one means the other loses). Because if the learner succeeds in leaving early without having worked, he's 'won' and the teacher has 'lost'; if the teacher succeeds in making him stay, the teacher 'wins' and the learner 'loses'. In other words, where there was potential for the teacher and learner to have a shared goal – successful learning – the situation shifts to one where they have directly conflicting goals.

- We can't say that Jaz is entirely unmotivated. He may not be motivated to learn, but something is clearly motivating him to avoid learning and to get out of that classroom.

From this analysis we can identify a number of questions that we need to answer before we decide which tactics to try.

- How can we prevent Jaz from undermining the motivation of the other learners?
- At what point did the possibility of a shared goal turn to conflict?
- How and where can we intervene to avoid this happening?
- What's driving Jaz? How can we best discover which of the Four Big Demotivators we're dealing with here?

So which alternative approach will be most useful in helping us to answer these questions? We already know he won't respond to the promise or withholding of Reward by the fact that he ignores the deal struck with the rest of the learners. At this stage, trying to engage his interest with a bit of Razzmatazz seems like a long shot. Based on what we know about his behaviour and responses so far, our best bet is probably the Relationship approach. Even if we can't engage him in work at this stage, we may be able to engage him in conversation. This is the simplest way to find out what's driving him. If it's his fear that he'll find the work too difficult, for example, we'll know to introduce some differentiation of task and/or assessment; we'll also know that pushing him hard to do something he's scared of is only going to make matters worse. The possibility of a shared goal disappeared when Jaz was first of all isolated and then left to his own devices while the teacher concentrated on supporting the learners whom she'd managed to motivate. It's not that she was 'wrong' to do this; after all, she had a responsibility to the majority. But it does illustrate very clearly how one approach is not enough. If his own fears were getting in the way of Jaz being motivated, being isolated and ignored would only exacerbate the problem. Just as any group of learners will contain people with different learning styles, so it will contain learners with different motivational needs.

Key points

- Motivating learners isn't a battle of wills. Keep your eye on the shared goal.
- If you can't engage the learner in work, engage him or her in conversation.
- In any group of learners there will be a diversity of motivational needs. Don't assume in your planning that one approach will work for all.

Motivating the learners that Razzmatazz won't reach

However carefully you handle it and whatever steps you take to avoid leaving learners feeling exposed or at risk, Razzmatazz won't work for everybody. Some learners – and you may be one of them – feel their heart sink when told they are going to take part in a lively, interactive activity, or play a learning game. Some people prefer to learn in more conventional ways, working through textbooks or web pages, listening to your input and taking notes. They tend to be in a minority in FE in the 14–19 age-group, and may well include individuals who feel delighted that you've finally got the rest of their class to sit up and listen, but who would rather watch all this from the sidelines while getting on quietly with their learning in their own way. So what do you do when your innovative approach is succeeding with almost – but not quite – everyone? Here are a number of tactics you can try:

- Appoint them to an observer's role in any activity where this a) will be interesting and worthwhile for them; b) can be justified in terms of attaching value to their feedback; and c) will involve other observers so that they are not singled out.

- Ask them to volunteer as one of the adjudicators or score-keepers in games, quizzes, competitions, etc.

- Wherever possible, give them a research or support role rather than a presentational or high-profile role.

- Manage group activities so that they are able to work with a group that will appreciate their contribution rather than ostracise them.

- Include in your lesson planning some differentiated activities that play to their strengths; for example, activities that involve note-taking, careful listening, accurate recall.

In this chapter we've looked at how we can focus in on the needs of individual learners who may not be responding to the motivational approach that's achieving its desired aim with the rest of their classmates. In the final section we're going to turn our attention to some of the questions that FE teachers most frequently raise in relation to motivating individual learners.

Trouble-shooting

How do I motivate someone to shut up and listen?

- Drop your voice and speak quietly.

- Refuse to make eye contact with them while they're talking.

- Say something unexpected/intriguing/contentious.

- Don't stand in one spot and talk. Move about the room and talk directly to the talkers from close up, but without invading their space (space invasion is confrontational).

How do I get someone to interact with me instead of with the other learners?

- Do or say something more interesting than the learners (but remember: it has to be something they *do* find interesting, not something we think they *should* find interesting!).

- Join their group and work with them.

- Manage the allocation of groups so that they're not with people they usually interact with.

- Don't make them sit at the front. That just gives them the ideal spot from which to turn and talk to the whole class.

How do I win someone over?

- Before you can get them to like you, you have to make them believe that you like them.

- Find something – anything – to praise them for, even if it's something they've done right by accident.

- Smile.

How do I persuade someone that learning is worth their while?

- Sell it to them! Tell them the ways that it's relevant to 'Real Life'.

- Point out some relevance to a field you know they dream of succeeding in, for example motor racing, rock star status, making lots of money.

How do I motivate someone to put their phone away?

- Make them unpopular if they don't, by making a deal with the class that they get extra break time but lose five minutes every time someone uses a phone or a phone rings.

- Have a visible phones policy: all phones switched off and exposed to view on tables/desks/benches.

- Pre-empt the 'emergency at home' argument by ensuring that every learner has the number of the college office on a card to leave at home in case of emergency, and assure them that the message *will* get through!

How do I motivate someone to join in with a group activity?

- Manage the group membership so that they're with a) people they want to work with; or b) people who'll encourage them to work.

- Give them a role that plays to their strengths or reflects their interests. For example, if they find it difficult to sit still, appoint them as the go-between who liaises between groups.

How do I know when the situation with a student has reached a point when it's no longer within my remit to try to handle it and I must refer it on?

- If his or her lack of motivation becomes violently confrontational.

- If you suspect the underlying problem may be drugs or alcohol abuse;

- If you suspect the lack of motivation is due to serious psychological problems;

- If you have good reason to suspect underlying problems at home, such as abuse, neglect, bereavement.

Summary

In this chapter we have discussed how individuals can be motivated and encouraged to join in with, rather than distract and demotivate, the rest of the group. We have seen that within any group of learners there will be a range of different motivational needs, and that we, as teachers, therefore need to develop a range of strategies to address these. Sometimes a process of trial and error is necessary before we discover what will work with any one individual. But, we have argued, this is almost always worthwhile, because the way we respond to that individual can have a big effect on the motivation of the rest of the group, particularly if we are dealing with a demotivated demotivator. Sometimes we'll be able to find an immediate tactic, such as tactically ignoring the postures or complaints of 'boredom'. Sometimes our approach will take a bit of strategic planning and may only begin to work over a series of lessons. Above all, we are most likely to succeed when we don't treat it as a battle to be won, but evade confrontation and keep our eye on the shared goal – the success of the learner.

7 Motivating 14–16-year-olds

The arrival of 14–16-year-olds in FE colleges was all about motivation. The 2005 White Paper 14–19 Education and Skills (London: DfES) explained that this initiative was based on the belief that learners who had not been motivated by the National Curriculum would find a vocational curriculum more inspiring. However, if it has been your experience that this is not always the case, you are not alone. In any case, as teachers we'd be unwise simply to depend on the curriculum alone to motivate our learners. We know already from previous chapters as well as from our own experience that motivation will depend heavily on at least two other factors:

- how the curriculum is taught
- how interactions are handled in the classroom or workshop.

What differentiates 14–16-year-olds from any other group of FE learners?

Some would argue that the answer to this is 'Nothing'; that making them into a special case does neither 14–16-year-olds nor their teachers any favours. But there are specific learner characteristics that we can attribute to 14–16-year-olds who find their way into FE, and these may provide us with some clues as to how to increase their motivation. These characteristics could include some or all of the following:

- They haven't responded productively to the learning experience provided by school.
- They may therefore have a concept of themselves as 'failures' when it comes to learning.
- They may have built up a negative perception of teachers.
- They may therefore have negative expectations of their relationship with you, the teacher.

- They may be defensive.

- They may have negative expectations of any formal learning experience.

- They may have a shorter attention span than older learners.

- They may find it difficult to adapt to the comparative freedoms of FE and may take undue advantage of these.

- They may find it difficult to adapt to the comparative freedoms of FE, perceive this as lack of structure and find it frightening.

- They are younger than the majority of FE learners, and may feel intimidated.

- They are unused to taking responsibility for their learning.

- Fourteen-year-olds will behave like 14-year-olds (which sometimes means behaving like six-year-olds).

That's a pretty daunting list. And you'll notice how many of those points relate to the Four Big Demotivators: Fear, Boredom, Previous Negative Experience and Loss of Hope, which we explored in Chapter 1. But don't let's forget that we're only describing some of the characteristics of those young learners who present as unmotivated. The 14-year-olds who come in to FE and take to it like a caterpillar to a cabbage leaf are the ones for whom the initiative is an immediate success. The learners we're talking about here are the ones who require a lot of hard work and ingenuity on the FE teacher's part before they begin to benefit from the second chance that this transition offers. And although we've just looked at a likely list of group characteristics, we also have to remember that within each group of 14–16-year-olds there will also be a range of individual needs.

Teaching with confidence

Now, let's give our attention to the teacher for a minute. We've looked at how the learners may be feeling, but the teacher, too, may be bringing some anxieties and preconceptions to the classroom or the workshop. If most of your prior experience has been of teaching learners aged 16+, you may well have doubts about your ability to do your best with this younger lot, and this in turn may affect the way you interact with them or interpret their behaviour. So we're talking here about your motivation, too. Because a teacher who lacks enthusiasm or confidence themselves will have difficulty motivating their learners, as we've already seen in earlier chapters.

Some positive steps

Here are some positive things we can do, then, to encourage and sustain the motivation of 14–16-year-old learners. They are tactics that will enable us to feel confident about supporting their learning. We'll list them first – a counterbalance to that daunting list of negatives with which we began this chapter – and then we'll go on to explore each one in terms of practical activities and examples. You'll notice as you read through them that there are tactics here that could prove equally useful with groups of 16–19-year-olds who have difficulty settling or concentrating.

- Provide clear structure and direction.

- Incorporate frequent changes of learner activity into your lesson plan.

- Begin the lesson with a 'settling' activity.

- Relate everything you can – including expectations about behaviour – to the work situation. After all, that's why they're in your class and not at school.

- Make the learning objectives of each activity clear before and after: This is what you're going to learn to do. . . This is what you've now learned to do.

- Provide worksheets and gapped handouts.

- Find ways to build their self-esteem.

- Find opportunities to give praise not only for their performance, but also for effort, behaviour and attitude.

- Reward individuals with prizes (e.g. sweets).

- Reward the whole class with Happy Time (e.g. ten minutes at the end of the lesson where you all play a game relevant to their learning).

- Build in frequent breaks.

- Make heavy use of Razzmatazz.

- Break tasks down into small steps so there are more opportunities for success and praise.

- Make sure any instructions you give are clear, and given one step at a time. And be prepared to repeat them as many times as it takes.

- Look enthusiastic.

- Be approachable.

- Maintain a routine (e.g. in the way you begin and end lessons).

- End the lesson positively, with a structured recap and praise or prizes for those who've earned them.

There's a lot to think about there, so let's take each one and unpack it a little more.

Provide clear structure and direction

In comparison with the school environment from which they have come, the more flexible regime of the college and the comparative anonymity of the individual learner may prove too much of a temptation for some young learners. The lack of apparent external constraints may appear to provide the opportunity to abandon thoughts of learning altogether. For others, the feeling of suddenly being a very small fish in a very large ocean may be so daunting that they become overwhelmed by that Big Demotivator, Fear, which we discussed in Chapter 1.

By providing structure and clear direction we address both of these potential demotivators. There are a number of ways we can do this:

- In every lesson tell them what they are going to do, do it, and then tell them what they've done!

- Give a clear time allowance for each task, a countdown as it proceeds ('Ten minutes left.' 'Five minutes left.' etc.), and a final and unambiguous signal that time is up.

- You can use an alarm clock as part of that last tactic for some novelty value and to really get their attention.

- Make college rules clear and take time to discuss them if necessary. Summarise them if needed (colleges sometimes have far too many for learners to keep in mind all at once). Uphold them consistently (e.g. if there's no food and drink to be brought into classrooms then there's no food and drink to be brought into classrooms. Ever. And that includes your cup of coffee.).

- Make or negotiate your own specific classroom rules if appropriate. Make them few, keep them simple and then stick to them.

- Make sure you abide by all the rules yourself.

- Be consistent and fair. Don't have 'moods' or obvious favourites.

- Make the aims of the course clear, and reiterate them every session if necessary.

- Establish a pattern to your lessons. This doesn't mean doing the same old activities every time. It means things like always starting at the same time (on time); beginning with a recap once they've settled down; always having breaks at the same time; always having a question time at the same point in the lesson, and so on.

Incorporate frequent changes of learner activity into your lesson plan

Younger learners can be restless and easily bored. Teachers often report that learners in this age group have a shorter attention span than older learners. They may need to move around more and expend some of that energy. Building frequent changes of activity – and the emphasis here is on *learner activity* – into your lesson plan can help accommodate this. For example:

- Keep teacher verbal inputs or 'mini-lectures' as brief as possible. It's better to have several short periods of exposition interspersed with periods of learner activity, than to expect 14–16-year-old learners to listen to you attentively for any length of time.

- Choose teaching and learning methods that involve active rather than passive learning; in other words, doing rather than listening and watching. If you don't plan something for them to do, they may end up doing something you didn't plan!

- In static, classroom lessons plan activities that allow for some movement (as far as Health and Safety allow). For example, if you have learners working in small groups, give a signal (whistle, gong, alarm clock) after five or ten minutes for one member of each group to move on to the next in order to share ideas and information. Or have a one-minute 'break' every 20 minutes where everyone stands up, rolls their shoulders or stretches, and sits down again.

- Use a soft ball or beanbag in question-and-answer sessions. Learners throw it to whoever they want to answer the next question.

Begin the lesson with a 'settling' activity

This achieves two things. It helps to establish an orderly routine, and it creates a relative quiet in which you can be heard. This is particularly important at the beginning of the lesson as this is where you give a recap of the last lesson, explain the objective of the present lesson, and give your initial input or instructions for the first task. We can't expect learners to be motivated if they can't hear what they're supposed to be doing, or if their initial impression of the lesson is one of noisy disorder. Settling activities can include:

- A question or puzzle on the board or screen. This might be a clue to the subject of the lesson.

- A wordsearch of key subject-specific terms.

- A challenge that assesses their retention of knowledge so far, for example 'Who can think of and write down five different kinds of. . .'

- A short, gapped handout, which they can fill in using knowledge/under-standing from the previous lesson.

- A five-minute YouTube clip with a question sheet to fill in afterwards.

You'll be able to think of many more such settling activities specific to your own subject area. The trick with a settling activity is to ensure that the learners are immediately occupied and engaged, so that the lesson doesn't begin in a messy way. It's a signal that says, 'This time is important. We have work to do.'

You may well have concerns that learners' lack of punctuality will wreck any plans you make for any kind of orderly initial activity. The tactic here is to ensure that you devise settling activities that the learners will want to participate in rather than avoid. That's why there's an emphasis in the list above on puzzles, games and entertainment. The idea is that the activities themselves become an incentive for learners to turn up on time.

Relate everything you can – including expectations about behaviour – to the work situation

These learners are in FE rather than at school because it's supposed that the emphasis on vocational education and skills will motivate them in a way that the school curriculum has not. This, then, is your trump card, and you should play it wherever and however you can. Be careful, however, not to play this card in such a way that you activate one of the Four Big Demotivators. This is easily done, and you'll need to be especially vigilant in order to avoid saying things like:

x 'You'll never be a plumber if you can't add up.' (Loss of Hope)
x 'You'll have to be quicker than that at work or they'll be on you like a ton of bricks.' (Fear)

x 'Boring? Of course it's boring. Get used to it. That's what it's like at work.' (Boredom)
x 'I don't expect miracles. You wouldn't be here doing this if you were any good at
learning stuff.' (Previous Negative Experience of learning)

You don't need to say any of that because there are lots of ways to use learners' expectations of the world of work as a positive motivator. For example:

✓ Begin by 'negotiating' rules of behaviour based on what would be acceptable in the workplace. You're at a distinct advantage here, as you're almost certainly going to be the only one with any credible experience of what is and what isn't acceptable. Therefore if you tell them that phones have to be switched off when they're working, who are they to argue? (Though of course they will.)

✓ Say things like: 'Now, when you're doing this at work what you'll need to do is. . .'

✓ Say things like: 'When you're at work you'll be doing this every day and you'll find you just keep getting better and better at it.'

✓ Explain Health and Safety rules in terms of the workplace: 'If we were at work, what would we have to do with these tools?' Or 'What might happen if we ran about in the salon?' Or 'How would we need to handle that if we were passing it to one of our colleagues on the ward?'

✓ Relate rules or advice on social skills and appropriate interactions to workplace situations: 'How would you need to say that if you were talking to a workmate in front of customers?' Or 'What might happen if you talked to somebody like that at work?'

✓ Help them to picture themselves as successful in the workplace: 'Watch carefully. One day you'll be showing somebody at work how to do this.'

✓ Utilise resources that relate to their vocational area of interest. For example, if you're teaching English GCSE to motor vehicle engineers, use an article from a motorbike website for comprehension questions; if you're teaching numeracy to learners in hairdressing, take your examples from timings for colourants or lengths of appointments.

✓ Play up your own vocational skills. Present yourself not only as a teacher (because they might associate teachers with previous negative experiences of learning), but also as an electrician or a hairdresser or a construction expert (obviously assuming that's what you really are. Because if you start telling them you were a catwalk model or that you served ten years with the SAS, or even that you managed to combine both these careers, they're going to start smelling a rat). Playing up your vocational expertise is more likely to give you the street cred you need to have them hanging on your every word (well, almost).

Make the learning objectives of each activity clear before and after

- Learners of all ages need to know *why* it is they're doing what they're doing; this is particularly important in the case of younger learners because they often take up the defensive attitude of 'Why should I?' or 'What's the point?' So you need to explain to them very clearly exactly what the point is; to do this, you have to be sure about it yourself.

- So it's a good idea before each activity to tell them, 'This is what you're going to learn to do...' When the activity is finished you can reinforce this by reiterating why they did it: 'So now, having learned that, you are able to...'

- If at the same time you take the opportunity to relate this to their vocational choice (see previous point) like this: 'This is what you're going to learn to do... because you'll need to be able to do this when you're an engineer/ hairdresser/chef...' then you're doubling your chances of getting them motivated.

- Don't just flash the lesson objectives up on the board and expect that to have the same effect. It won't.

Provide worksheets and gapped handouts

The main reason you'll need to do this is that most 14–16-year-olds coming into FE won't arrive with note-taking skills. So if you want to make sure they have a note of key points or important diagrams or anything else, you'll have to provide worksheets and handouts, either in hard copy or online on the college intranet. However, a handout is of absolutely no use at all if the learner doesn't read it first and then save it for future revision. So here are some things you can do to increase the chances of that happening.

- Make sure worksheets and web pages aren't overcrowded with information. Only include what's really important, preferably in bullet-point format.

- Make them easy to read by using large-ish (e.g. 16-point) font and spacing out each point clearly.

- Use pictures (and colours if that's feasible) to draw the attention.

- Choose your language carefully. These learners may well not yet be familiar with the specialised language of their vocational choice. Using words or expressions they don't understand will turn them off immediately.

- Don't give them too many pages of information in any one lesson. Think how you yourself feel in meetings where you have to suffer 'death by handout'.

- Don't give out hard copies just before you need the class to listen to you or watch what you're doing or concentrate on anything else at all. The last thing you want to find yourself doing is telling them NOT to read a handout!

- When you do give them out, take time to go through the handout with them, asking and answering questions as you go. That way you know they've read them through at least once.

- If you're giving out hard copies, make sure the handouts are hole-punched so that they can be put safely in the learners' files at the end of the lesson and not creased and crumpled at the bottom of their sports bag.

- Refer to past handouts now and again in subsequent lessons. Say, 'Now, let's take another look at that information I put on the VLE last week, headed Three Basic Rules.' If you establish this as a regular practice, the learners will get the hang of the fact that what you're giving them is important and central to their learning.

- Gapped handouts are very useful for motivating learners to listen. If you're explaining something to them, for example, or showing them a brief YouTube clip or presentation, you can get them to listen for and fill in the missing words or phrases or percentages. Because this can be presented as a sort of game it can be surprisingly successful. The completed handouts can then be referred to subsequently as in the point above.

- Always check completed handouts before learners file them, to ensure that the information they've now got down in black and white is correct. The read-through stage is particularly important with gapped handouts (see above).

Find ways to build their self-esteem

There are lots of ways to do this. Taking the time to talk to them as individuals; looking as though you're pleased to see them; admiring their phone case/boots/

tattoos/piercing; asking their advice about racing bikes if you know they like bike racing. Even the most brash behaviour can be a cover for lack of confidence, so don't worry too much about giving them an inflated view of themselves. They're youngsters new to a big institution. If learners get the impression you like having them there, they're more likely to be motivated to listen to what you say and do some work for you. Of course, all these conversational gambits require you to have learned a bit about the learners as individuals – and enable you to learn more.

Find opportunities to give praise not only for their performance, but also for behaviour and attitude

You can praise them for getting to your class on time, for adhering to the behaviour code, for doing something you've asked them to do (such as give out handouts). You can even praise them for things they didn't even know they were doing, such as letting you go through a door first when you've beaten them to it anyway, or getting quickly into a group when actually they haven't really had to shift their seat much at all. And you can extend this to praising them for offering to answer a question even when they really haven't, as long as you don't expose them by asking them for the answer: 'I can see Taylor smiling, so I know she knows the answer to this one. Let's see who else knows. . .' Of course, Taylor may well contradict you, but she'll get a taste of being praised and just might be motivated to earn some next time. The thing about this sort of praise is that it challenges learners' preconceived notions about themselves and their achievements as not being praiseworthy. If you believe nothing you do will earn you praise, you'll look for other ways to gain attention, such as disruptive or challenging behaviour. But once learners recognise that praise is within their grasp, they might just go for it. Not always, but often enough to make this tactic worth a try.

Reward individuals with prizes (e.g. sweets)

We talked extensively about using Reward in Chapter 2. This strategy can be used quite straightforwardly for 14–16-year-olds. For example:

- Throwing a sweet, raisins or other small prize to someone who gives a correct answer.

- Playing Pass the Parcel: whoever has the parcel when the music stops has the chance to answer a question for a prize.

- Having a prize-giving at the end of the lesson for the learner or learners who've worked hardest. You could decide the winner yourself or ask the learners to nominate someone.

These tactics might appear a bit 'childish' or even patronising; but in fact the fun element works well with learners of all ages. For the 14–16 age-group it can work on a number of levels. Learners who think they can't possibly have fun while learning find these expectations confounded; and learners who have previously used disruption to draw attention find that they can draw even more by engaging with their learning. This is all about providing a 'pay-off' that – from the learners' point of view – makes learning worthwhile. Although you are hoping that in the longer term they will discover that learning is worthwhile in itself, the strategy of rewarding with prizes is a way of jump-starting this process.

Reward the whole class with Happy Time (e.g. ten minutes at the end of the lesson where you all play a 'game')

You might want to find a different name for this if you think it sounds too much like time for cheap drinks, or if you want the learners to think of the whole lesson as Happy Time. But whatever you call it, it can be a very effective way of motivating this age-group, particularly if you knock time off it for time lost in the lesson through individuals' off-task behaviour or non-cooperation. Then it becomes a way of exerting peer pressure: 'Nadine, remember that for every minute you spend playing with your phone everyone's going to be losing a minute off.'

Happy Time. The sort of activities Nadine could be causing the group to miss are up to you, as long as they are:

- fun for the learners
- related to their learning so that it's not time wasted.

For example, you could play Hangman on the board, or via the data projector, as this can be seen by the learners as a non-learning 'treat' while in fact it's developing their spelling, vocational vocabulary, cooperation and team skills.

Build in frequent breaks

This is a good way of addressing a couple of major issues: learners' attention span and the physical restlessness of young learners. Breaks can also be used in the same way as Happy Time (see previous point), with minutes deducted for time lost through individual non-cooperation in lessons. They can also be extended by a minute or two to reward group cooperation or good work.

Because there is an issue about the supervision of younger learners, you will need to restrict these breaks to the classroom or workshop rather than let the learners go wandering. But three minutes' Talk Time or Check Your Texts Time twice during an hour's lesson is a Reward, which younger learners value and will usually be motivated to work for. Of course, if they regard the entire lesson anyway as Talk and Check Your Texts Time, this tactic won't work. But teachers who provide these small breaks report that they work well to channel off-task behaviour into those specific time slots.

Make heavy use of Razzmatazz

Loretta Starr would make a great teacher of 14–16-year-olds. Learning activities that are fun and attention-grabbing are ideal for this age-group, particularly those who've convinced themselves that learning is 'boring'. To remind yourself of some Razzmatazz ideas look again at Chapter 5. But always bear in mind that younger learners are very easily embarrassed and may be reluctant to take part in some activities that often go down well with older learners, such as role-play or stand-up debates. Group activities where no one individual learner feels 'exposed' may be the best idea.

Break tasks down into small steps

This is important if we want to make sure that learners a) understand what it is they're required to do; and b) are able to do it successfully. Most tasks can be broken down in this way, not only the most complex ones. This tactic doesn't necessarily call for all learners to be working at the same pace; it can still allow for differentiation. What it does mean is that no learners are pushed to proceed to the next step until they are secure in their achievement of the current one. In other words it avoids setting individuals up to fail – because no one's going to be motivated by the prospect of inevitable failure, are they?

Make sure any instructions you give are clear, and given one step at a time. And be prepared to repeat them as many times as it takes

We should add to this, 'And make sure that you are heard.' Clear, step-by-step instructions are important for all the same reasons set out in the point above. But you need to make sure the instructions are successfully communicated. This may mean:

- Having them written up on the board/via the data projector/on a flip chart. This is particularly important if there's a lot of ambient noise in the class.
- Going over the instructions, asking and answering questions about them until you're as certain as you can be that everyone understands them. And then. . .
- . . . moving around the room from individual to individual to check progress and understanding.
- Demonstrating patience by being prepared to repeat the instructions as many times as it takes. This is not to say, however, that you should keep repeating yourself when no one's listening. You repeat yourself because they're listening but don't yet get it.
- Finding different ways of saying the same thing if learners are having difficulty understanding. For example, relate it to something they'll be familiar with: 'Did you see *Top Gear* last night where someone had to check the timings for. . .? Well, what I need you to do is. . .'
- Being prepared to consider the possibility that you're not explaining it very well.

Look enthusiastic

If you don't look happy to be teaching them, how can you expect them to feel happy about being taught? And, strangely enough, on those occasions you have to go in there faking enthusiasm, you'll often find yourself beginning to feel the genuine thing. This is because you'll be picking up the learners' positive responses to the way you're acting towards them. In other words, looking enthusiastic can motivate you as well as the learners.

Be approachable

There are three very good reasons to be approachable:

1   Learners will be more likely to want to please or impress you if they like you.

2   If learners are scared of you, you're playing into the hands of that Big Demotivator, Fear.

3 We've seen (in Chapter 3) how the Relationship between teacher and learners can be a central issue when it comes to motivation. Being approachable is part of building that positive Relationship.

Remember that being approachable is not the same thing as being 'one of the gang'. You're not the learners' friend; they already have their friends. You're their teacher. And if you're going to support their learning successfully, that's what they need you to be.

Maintain a routine (e.g. in the way you begin and end lessons)

This relates closely to the first point in this long list, about providing structure. Routines can make learners feel safe. A settling activity at the beginning and a recap and prize-giving at the end help to provide the structure and routine within which learners have the sense of security and structure they need in order to engage with their learning.

End the lesson positively, with a structured recap and praise or prizes for those who've earned them

Positive endings are especially important. They are the last impression learners will take away from the lesson, and are therefore the best trigger to get learners to attend willingly next time. It's also important that the lesson ends with a sense of order and achievement, and not with bustle and chaos and learners packing their bags several minutes before the end, ready to make a dash for it. That only reinforces the idea that they're there under duress.

Summary

We've looked at a whole range of strategies for motivating 14–16-year-olds. Many of them will also prove useful for motivating older learners. They can be tried separately or in combination. They aren't all guaranteed to work all of the time with all classes; but they do provide a repertoire on which you can draw to find something that works – as a one-off or on a regular basis – for you and your learners. But although we've been talking in this chapter about 14–16-year-old learners in collective terms, we must also remember that, although there are shared or group characteristics, which we can learn to address, each learner will also have his or her own individual motivational needs.

8 Motivating adult learners

Ade walks into the classroom and tries to put on a bit of a swagger. He glances around at the other learners. They all look much more confident than he feels. Some of them even seem to know one another already although this is the first day of the course. He has no idea what this is going to be like. He hopes it's not going to be like school, because he hated school and he's pretty sure none of the teachers liked him. He hopes there's not going to be a lot of reading to do. What if he's asked to read something out loud? He goes cold just thinking about it. He smiles his best smile and takes a seat near the back, next to someone who looks like she knows what she's doing. If the worst comes to the worst he can sneak a look at what she's doing and copy it. And if the worst comes to the very worst, he can always pack it in and just not turn up tomorrow. 'Hi!' he says cheerily. 'I'm Ade.'

Leah smiles briefly at Ade and looks away. 'Oh, God,' she's thinking, 'here's another one. Not a care in the world. What am I doing here? I shouldn't be here. They all know what they're doing. They all know stuff I don't know. What if I get asked to say something? I'm going to look stupid. I shouldn't have come. What made me think I could do this?'

Ade and Leah are both in their thirties and this is an Access to HE class. They are both hoping eventually to study for a degree. Given their acute state of nerves on this first day, we can begin to get some idea of the powerful sense of motivation they must have had to get them to this point where they have made the commitment to enrol and turn up. And we also get some insight into how easily that motivation could be destroyed or undermined. And it's quite probable that every other learner in that classroom – however confident and worldly wise they may appear – is feeling something similar. The danger is that we, as teachers, may take that apparent confidence at face value and inadvertently make demands or comments that have a negative or even destructive impact.

However, there are *some* assumptions that it is useful to make about adult learners:

- They are often not as confident as they appear.

- There is a powerful sense of motivation there that got them to return to learning, and which can be sustained and built upon.

- As adults they have responsibilities, commitments and demands on their time quite apart from their college work.

- Necessarily these other commitments and demands will sometimes take priority in their lives.

- As a consequence we can't just assume that the strong motivation that brought them to college in the first place will automatically keep them there if we don't recognise and address their motivational needs.

There's a common assumption by those outside FE that teaching and motivating adults must be a doddle, but we know this is quite mistaken. Certainly it can often be a pleasure. But teaching is never 'easy', whatever the group, and we still need strategies to motivate adult learners, even though this will sometimes mean changing or adapting the tactics that we would use with 14–19-year-olds.

Fear, Previous Negative Experience and the adult returner

Further Education has traditionally been the sector of the second chance, providing an opportunity to re-engage with learning for people who weren't able, for one reason or another, to make the most of their compulsory education. We refer to them as 'adult returners' for the obvious reason that they are *returning* to education or training. But this return may well carry with it a number of misgivings. Ade and Leah were expressing most of them. What will it be like to be back in the classroom? What if the work's too hard? What sort of standard is expected? Might they be expected to know everything just because they're an adult? What if everyone else in the class knows more than they do or is cleverer than they are? Despite their apparent confidence, the adult learner may be genuinely scared. And of course we know from Chapter 1 that fear is one of the Big Demotivators.

While the motivation that drove the adult returner to enrol in FE is an indication that he or she is less likely to be stumbling over barriers like Boredom or Loss of Hope, the other Big Demotivator that an adult learner might well become a victim of Previous Negative Experience. Look at Ade. He reminds us that adult learners can bring with them a history of difficult teacher–learner relationships; or memories of being a 'failure'; or a past in which learning has been associated with boredom, marginalisation or punishment. None of this is necessarily evident in the adult's confident and chatty demeanour. But the memory of negative experiences may lie just beneath the surface, easily reawakened by unconstructive feedback or an abrupt word from you or me.

In these times when we are encouraged to see lifelong learning as the norm – when the rate of technological advance creates the need for regular re-skilling and updating, and when there is concern over the level of vocational qualifications and basic skills in the adult population – it's more important than ever that we should find ways to keep adult learners motivated once they have taken that step of enrolling themselves on their chosen course. The snapshot we had at the beginning of the chapter of how Ade and Leah were feeling on their first day would have been the same whether they were enrolling on a basic skills programme, a Level 2 in construction, an Advanced Level programme or a foundation degree. And, as we know, any self-doubts and anxieties they have will probably stay with them long beyond that first session. One of our responsibilities as teachers is to remember that, and to make sure it informs the way we plan and support their learning.

We can summarise all this in the following rule of thumb:

The adult learner should be treated as more vulnerable to demotivation than he or she might, on the surface, appear to be.

Goal-orientation

Another key characteristic of adult learners is that they usually know exactly what it is they want when they enrol at college. They have a goal in mind, and are often making considerable sacrifices, in terms of finance or family time, in order to achieve it. This is a huge investment, and means they will want value for their time and money.

Their goal-orientation is also likely to mean that they are hungry for structure and input, and could well become demotivated if these are not to be found. In order to keep adult learners motivated it is useful to incorporate the following strategies into your planning:

- **Provide a clearly organised programme, and stick to it.** Give them a structured timetable for the term, semester or year, so that they can see what they'll be doing week by week and where the assessments and hand-in dates are scheduled. Adults often have hectic lives and family responsibilities. Their time is rarely their own. They need plenty of advance warning of deadlines and key dates.

- **Explain clearly the expected learning outcomes for each session**. Adult learners will usually pull with you if they know where they're supposed to be going. It's also a good idea to review the outcomes at the end of the lesson in order to emphasise what the learners have achieved and confirm for them that their time has been well spent.

- **Make the assessment criteria clear, make sure they all have copies and link any assessment feedback clearly to those criteria**. Adult learners need to know exactly how they are doing and what they need to do to improve. Although this is true of all learners, adults tend to take more responsibility for improving their own performance, and therefore need to be provided with the measures to do this.

- **Start on time and don't finish early!** While younger learners may regard an early finish as a Reward, adult learners may well feel cheated if they don't get their money's worth. And having made the effort to turn out and turn up, they won't appreciate hanging about for a delayed start, or packing up an hour early to go home.

- **Maintain an orderly classroom.** Adults are generally less likely to present you with challenging or disruptive behaviour. But if you teach adults and younger learners together in a mixed group, you will need to ensure that the behaviour of the younger ones doesn't disrupt the learning of the others. More easily said than done, perhaps. But in a situation such as this you will find yourself having to address the motivation of the 16–19-year-olds in order to maintain the motivation of the adults. This is where some of those ideas from Chapters 1 to 5 come in handy.

- **Choose high-intensity methods**. As well as being hungry for structure, adult learners are also hungry for input. Although individual preferred learning styles will differ, most adults will expect plenty of time-effective teacher activity. In other words, they'll want to leave the lesson feeling their time was well spent and that they know much more than when they came in. This doesn't mean that you have to stick exclusively to time-effective methods such as lectures, demonstrations, and question and answer. But, used appropriately, methods like these will help satisfy adult learners' need to feel 'well-fed'.

Relationship and motivation

We saw in Chapter 3 how the relationship between teacher and learner can be a major factor in terms of the learner's motivation. This is no less true of adult learners. However, the ways in which the relationship is expressed will inevitably be rather different. For example, we probably wouldn't feel as comfortable taking a parental or 'big sisters' tone with an adult as we might with a 14–19-year-old. On the other hand, straying over into the role of best buddy is no more appropriate with an adult than it is with a younger learner. The relationship is still that of teacher and learner. So if, for example, we are aiming to motivate with praise, we have to find a way of giving praise that doesn't sound patronising. And if we're hoping to motivate through building a positive relationship, we have to find ways of relating that are appropriate in a professional working context. So where we might usefully say to a 16-year-old, 'If you don't concentrate and finish that task, you're going to miss five minutes of your break,' and justifiably expect this to motivate her to get on with it, the same admonition to an adult learner could well be construed as an insult to her dignity and result in her never attending your classes again.

So some good pointers to bear in mind when aiming to motivate adults are:

- When giving positive feedback, make sure you're communicating adult to adult. For example, 'Right. Well done. Thank you' is obviously going to work a lot better with an adult than, 'Good girl!', or 'Yes. What a clever chap' – and should avoid a punch on the nose for being patronising.

- Rules that work well to motivate younger learners by imposing a sense of order will sometimes prove counter-effective when applied to adults. For example, imagine saying to a 45-year-old, 'Put your hand up if you want to answer a question.'

- Younger learners are liable to arrive late and want to leave early. Adult learners may well arrive early or hang about after the lesson and expect your undivided attention in a one-to-one conversation about the course, their problems, or the meaning of life. In other words, adult learners can present as surprisingly needy. You need to find ways of dealing with this. Either resign yourself to hiding in the toilets or losing your three-minute lunch break, or – if you're serious about keeping these learners motivated – consider scheduling the last ten minutes of each session to see learners on an individual basis. The alternative – making the learners feel avoided and rejected – risks seriously undermining their motivation.

Adult life and responsibilities

Adult learners' commitments and responsibilities outside college mean that you'll need to develop a flexible response to timings and deadlines. If you don't, you run the risk of the learner just giving up, deciding it's too much hassle trying to fit college and home life together. Your flexible response might include:

- Agreeing for those with childcare responsibilities to arrive late or leave early.

- Being flexible about the start time for everyone, and imposing no sanctions for lateness. This will mean choosing an activity for the opening of the lesson that latecomers can catch up with in their own time, for example revision exercises, reading, inviting learners to ask questions. But remember, it has to be an activity that motivates those who can arrive on time! And *you* should *always* ensure you're there on time, for the reasons we gave earlier.

- Avoiding wherever possible the imposition of large amounts of obligatory homework.

- Providing references to online sources of information and other key resources wherever possible and not expecting learners to divert their limited time and resources away from feeding their children and into trawling the internet or even buying books!

- Having empathy for their current situation and treating them as you yourself would wish to be treated in the same circumstances (for example, in giving extended deadlines for coursework where there are genuine reasons to do so).

The learner as resource

Unlike the 14–19-year-old, the adult learner arrives in FE carrying a substantial weight of life experience. This can be a very valuable resource and should be factored into your lesson planning at every opportunity. By acknowledging learners' experience and expertise you will raise their confidence and increase their motivation. You don't have to ask them to deliver a treatise on a particular topic or put them on the spot, because you can acknowledge or draw on their experience in quite small ways. For example:

- Prefixing remarks with, 'As you may know...' or 'As some of you will know better than I do...' or 'Here's something some of you will already be familiar with...'

- Not always setting yourself up as the sole source of knowledge or expertise, but being prepared to defer to a learner who may have more recent experience or more detailed knowledge of a particular issue or procedure.

- Showing a genuine interest in what the learners may be able to add to the lesson from their own experience.

- Not making them jump through hoops. For example, requiring an adult learner on a health and social care course who has four children of her own to 'learn' to bath babies by watching you bath a plastic doll is not going to convince her that she's learning anything very valuable. So get her to show the rest how it's done.

Diversity

Further Education is a sector that prides itself on responding to diversity by accommodating a very wide range of learners and learning needs. The diversity of adult learners in FE is a good illustration of this, in terms of ability, goals, previous qualifications and motivational needs. They'll have some things in common as we've seen – juggling the busy lives and feeling some trepidation about returning to learning – but they'll have diverse needs when it comes to specific strategies for confidence building and motivation. At one extreme will be those who need to be credited with the ability to work autonomously and/ or creatively, and who may become demotivated if you bombard them with advice and exert too tight a control. At the other extreme will be adults who need exactly those sort of tight parameters and constant guidance in order to feel confident and motivated. In practical terms, this calls for a flexibility of approach.

Motivating by giving high levels of autonomy	Motivating by giving high levels of support
Providing the opportunity to undertake research or independent study.	Providing plenty of one-to-one help and tuition.
Setting longer-term, complex tasks such as assignments and reports, which give free rein to the learner's interest.	Setting observable tasks that allow you to give immediate feedback and encouragement.
Providing lectures and seminars and stressing the learner's own responsibility for note-taking.	Breaking tasks down into clearly defined steps and providing plenty of opportunity for practice.

'Gurus' from the world of work

When we're looking for ideas for motivating adult learners we can usefully draw on some of the strategies suggested by 'gurus' of the business world for motivating professionals in the workplace. Charles Handy, for example (Handy, 1993), suggests the following:

- Adults often find it motivating to be given some degree of autonomy in their work. So you could encourage adult learners to make their own decisions wherever possible, for example on their choice of topic or approach when it comes to projects and coursework.

- We need to build people's self-concept in order to get them to achieve high performance. This means giving adult learners plenty of positive feedback and praise, so that they begin to think of themselves as 'winners'.

- If we want to keep people motivated, we must avoid giving them a role or task that is incompatible with the way they see themselves in terms of their values, their position in society or their ambitions. For example, we should avoid teaching methods or learning activities that require learners to appear undignified or go against genuinely held beliefs, and we should never address them in a manner that appears to undermine their adult status.

- High expectations can create self-fulfilling prophecies, so we should always demonstrate to adult learners that we believe in them and have faith that they'll succeed.

Four Rs

How might our Four Big Motivators work with adult learners like Ade and Leah? Certainly we will have to use these motivators rather differently from the way we would with 14–19-year-olds.

1. Reward

If we want to motivate adults:

- Praise and positive attention will be more effective than sweets and prizes.
- Providing them with a sense of achievement will work better than letting them go early.

- The withholding of rewards, if used, needs to be handled with extreme care. For example, you might motivate an adult who talks too much to shut up and listen by withholding eye-contact when he or she is talking, but you wouldn't threaten sanctions such as the loss of a break.

2. Rules and Respect

If we want to motivate adults:

- We must remember that too much emphasis on rules can stifle adult creativity. A more constructive approach is to build trust.
- Giving them due respect for their status as adults may mean exercising extreme sensitivity and tact (as well as accuracy and honesty) in giving feedback on incorrect answers or inadequate work.
- We need to ensure that there's a sense of order and structure. This can mean taking responsibility to ensure that classroom disruption is kept to a minimum.

3. Relationship

If we want to motivate adults:

- We need to establish our authority without appearing patronising.
- We need to acknowledge their life experience without being condescending.
- We need to retain the responsibilities of teacher to learner without emphasising the inevitable power relations between our respective roles.
- We need to arrange the seating (where appropriate) to emphasise an equality of adult status. Horseshoe, hollow square or boardroom arrangements are ideal. Seating adults in rows as though they're back at school is not a good idea.

4. Razzmatazz

If we want to motivate adults:

- Our choice of teaching and learning methods must take account of adult behaviours and responses. For example, choose formal debates rather than competitions based on the current music craze.

- Choose role-play and simulation to allow adults to demonstrate existing skills and expertise. But never push or cajole those who are reluctant to join in.

- Try introducing some negotiation. What teaching methods do they prefer?

- Don't recreate school – in methods, authoritarian approach or seating arrangement.

Summary

For all adult learners their experience of FE has the potential to be literally life-changing. Their decision to come to college, to re-enter education or training, is usually made for just that reason. They are looking for something to change their lives. So whether they are enrolling on a Level 2 vocational programme or on a foundation degree, it's likely that an enormous amount of hope is being invested in this step. What we have to remember is that where expectations are so high, disappointment can hit hard, and cause motivation to evaporate in no time at all. This chapter has looked at some of the strategies we can employ to avoid this happening.

9 Selling maths and English

'From August 2014 students who have not achieved a good pass in English and/or maths by age 16 must continue towards achieving these qualifications... as a condition of student places being funded.'

(Written statement to Parliament by the Minister of State for Skills and Enterprise, 2 July 2014)

Ever had someone at your door trying to sell you something you just don't want? Well, if you've been recently involved with the provision of GCSE English and maths resits for FE learners, you'll know exactly how that salesperson feels, left standing there, smile fading, as the front door shuts in their face. When it comes to difficulties with motivation, the English and maths issue tops the lot. And this is completely understandable. For many learners, this requirement to resit subjects that they already associate with a sense of failure inevitably triggers *all four* of the Big Demotivators.

- **Fear**: No one likes to feel a failure. They've had that experience once and they're understandably reluctant to be put through it again. They may also, in relation to these subjects, have experienced being on the receiving end of teachers' or classmates' frustration, anger, contempt or derision. They have experienced mockery from their classmates. They don't want to think of themselves as a failure. They're scared that they're going to have to face all that again.

- **Boredom**: They haven't come into FE to do what they see as 'schoolwork'. They've come for vocational education and training. They don't want to have to sit through English and maths sessions that they associate with the 'boring' side of the school curriculum – and all the more so if they've struggled with one or both of these subjects and therefore can't imagine they could ever find them interesting. So the very idea of having to do maths and/or English again only sets up the expectation of hours of boredom.

- **Previous negative experience**: They've failed at this once. They experienced that failure as painful. It undermined their confidence. If they failed once, why would they succeed this time? For them, these subjects are associated with overwhelmingly negative feelings, which they strongly resent having to revisit.

- **Loss of hope**: They've finally escaped school and got into college, ready for a new start, ready to leave behind all the things about school that made them feel they were 'second best', 'a bit of a failure', 'not the brightest'. Maybe at college they'll be able to show what they can really do – show what they're good at – rebuild their confidence and self-esteem. But what's this? They've got to go on reliving their failure at English and/or maths? Oh. So not really a new start, then. Not really a clean slate. And it seems now they're stuck with taking these subjects over and over until they get them, which they don't feel they have a hope in hell of ever doing.

Because we're dealing here with the Big Four, all the strategies we've explored in Chapters 2 to 5, based on Reward, Relationships, Respect, Rules and Razzmatazz, will come in very useful. But, because the resits are such an overwhelming issue, for teachers as well as learners, we're going to look at wider ways in which we can address motivation particularly in this specific part of the curriculum. This chapter isn't about the practicalities and requirements of the English and maths curriculum nor is it about whether to embed or not embed, it's about the motivational issues that have made this English and maths requirement such a nightmare for some teachers and colleges.

What did the Romans ever do for us?

There's a scene in the classic Monty Python film, *Life of Brian*, where a group of amateurish insurgents are sitting around moaning about the Roman Empire that is currently occupying their country. One of the insurgents grumblingly asks, 'What have they ever given us?' There's a lot of nodding in agreement. Then someone pipes up, 'Except for the aqueduct.' Still grumbling and nodding, others begin to chip in: 'Yes, except for Sanitation. The Roads. Irrigation. Medicine. Education. Law and order. Public health. Peace. Even wine. Yes. Apart from those, what have they ever done for us?'

It's a great scene (you can find it on YouTube) and behind the humour is a serious point. It's easy to get up in arms about something and put up every resistance to it because it makes us feel bad, but if we stop for a moment and think it through, it's possible we'll begin to realise that it could offer us opportunities we might want to take advantage of.

Sly Cunningham – that cunning exponent of motivation through Reward – has this to say:

I'm involved in our English and maths provision in two ways. Like most of my colleagues, I'm required to embed the relevant skills in my vocational classes. But I also take some groups specifically for maths as part of the provision for those who need extra support. I'm a great believer in motivating through rewards and sanctions, and the thing about reward is that it doesn't necessarily have to be immediate. If you can encourage learners to recognise the longer-term rewards for doing something like getting the required grade in maths, you can begin to jumpstart their motivation. What I do, right at the beginning, when they're moaning and saying, 'What's the point? What's a good grade at maths GCSE ever done for anybody?' I take their question seriously and I spend a good part of the first session helping them to discover the answer. They're not used to their objections and questions being taken seriously, most of them. So when I show I'm willing to spend time listening to them and that I treat their question as a genuine one worth exploring, they see this as a sort of reward in itself. And when they do look into it, doing a bit of online research with help and support from me, they begin to find out for themselves exactly what a good GCSE in maths can do for them: all the jobs and career paths it can open the door to, the wider choice of routes through the qualifications system, the opportunities for employment abroad and so on. Once we've filled the board with these serious answers to their initial question, we've established the incentive for them to put some effort in. I'm not saying it's all plain sailing after that, I have to pull out every reward and sanction trick in my book to keep them on track, but it has proved a useful start with most of the groups. And one other thing: when I'm talking to the learners I don't refer to our lesson as 'maths'. Most of them have become conditioned to switch off at the very mention of maths. I call our lessons 'The Numbers Game' and I get them to use that name, too. They can take that any way they want but the advantage for me (and them) is I'm not having to battle quite so much against their idea that having to retake maths is somehow a punishment for them not having got it in the first place. I don't want them to regard the entire lesson as one big sanction – otherwise I'm never going to get through to them.'

The hard sell

What Sly's doing here is the hard sell. Like the salesperson on the doorstep, he's pointing out the potential rewards and the potential payback the learners could get for the investment of their time and energy. And he's good at it. He doesn't, according to him, get the door slammed in his face. 'Selling' English and maths is not just something the subject specialists need to do; all teachers of 16–19-year-olds will find this worth doing. Telling 16-year-olds that they have to do these subjects because it's now a government requirement certainly isn't going to get them motivated. And letting them see that you think it's a pretty daft idea, too, is likely to make them disengage altogether. But encouraging them to find out what could be in it for them, what the rewards could be only a little way down the line, is much more likely to help overcome some of their resistance.

And Sly's ploy of 'renaming' the subject is worth considering, too. This could also be part of the hard sell. If consumers grow tired of a product, or it somehow falls into disrepute, manufacturers will sometimes change the name. They'll 'rebrand' it so that it's no longer associated with something buyers have negative feelings about or have grown bored with. By encouraging his learners to call maths 'The Numbers Game', Sly is giving them a new way of seeing it. The word 'game' has positive associations and holds the promise of enjoyment and reward.

What's the story?

Each learner embarking on English and/or maths retakes will have their own story about these subjects, and, inevitably, it will be one that ends in failure. No wonder they want to draw a line under it and write 'The End'. All their relationships around English and maths will be tainted by that failure; their relationship with the teachers who taught them, with the parents or carers who expected more of them and, above all, with the subject itself. It's very difficult, therefore, when they find themselves about to be put through the whole thing again, to persuade them that this time it's possible – even, with a bit of hard work, likely – that the story could end very differently.

In Chapter 3 we saw how Davit Deera based his motivational techniques around building positive relationships. So how might he apply this approach to learners who have experienced a Loss of Hope of the possibility that their relationship with English and/or maths could ever end happily?

What I do, right from the start if I can, is to invite in some of the learners from the previous year who were successful with their retakes and get them to tell their stories. Their stories always begin in a way this year's group can relate to, such as struggling with the subject at school, switching off, doing badly, not liking the teacher or feeling bored or confused in the lessons. And I see this year's group nodding. They're thinking, 'Yes, that's me. That's exactly how it was with me.' And then last year's learner will tell how miserable they felt when they discovered they had to go through all that again with resits. And the group are still nodding. And then they get to hear what happened next. I choose my story-tellers carefully; they're all youngsters the new kids can relate to. They don't come over as 'try'ards' or teacher's pets. So when they talk about finding the college approach different from school, finding out how English or maths turned out to be important components of their vocational skills set, or discovering the subjects could be challenging in a good way, the new retake kids keep listening – mostly. And then comes the punch line, the story ending happily with a pass at a good grade, and all the opportunities that's opened up for them, how much better they feel about themselves and how they now really can write 'The End' under the story of their struggle. 'If I can do it, you can do it' is what they're saying and it's amazing how encouragement like that from their peers has so much more impact on learners than any amount of coaxing from a teacher.'

Happily ever after

Davit's strategy makes a lot of sense. It's good for the self-esteem of last year's successful learners, too, to be able to tell their story. However, it's a strategy that has to be handled with care. Hearing about the success of others can have a discouraging effect if not managed appropriately and not all young people will feel comfortable about telling their story. It's vital to the success of Davit's strategy that the chosen story-tellers are able to make it absolutely clear that they started from exactly the same position that this year's learners now find themselves: estranged from the subject by their Previous Negative Experience and dreading having to go through it all again. What they are there to show them is simply, 'Look, it can be done.' And, on a more subtle level, 'I listened to this teacher and he helped me to succeed.' In this way, Davit's approach is designed to mend learners' relationship, not only with the dreaded subject but also with the dreaded teacher!

Challenging mindset

One of the major problems with the English and maths resits, as we've seen, is that past failure has left learners with the firm belief these are subjects at which they can never succeed, so there's no point in trying. Carol Dweck, in her book, *Mindset: How you can Fulfil your Potential* (Robinson, 2012), explains that the beliefs we hold about our own skills, abilities or intelligence can be self-limiting. That is, they can prevent us from trying to develop our full potential. This can apply to teachers as well as learners. If we think, 'Oh, I'm no good at behaviour management. I'll never be any good at it,' we are displaying a fixed mindset – the belief that we would only be able to succeed at something if we already had a talent for it and that no amount of reading about it and practice will make any difference. When a learner says, 'I'm rubbish at maths, no point trying again, I won't get it,' their fixed mindset is preventing them from seeing that some effort or hard work might make all the difference. If they say, 'I hate English', that's displaying a fixed mindset about what they will and won't find enjoyable or rewarding. They hated it at school, so they're convinced they'll hate it at college. And forever after.

Loretta Starr, with her Razzmatazz approach (see Chapter 5), is well equipped to help learners break through this sort of fixed mindset and develop a growth mindset instead. A growth mindset is one in which we realise that we can develop and improve our abilities, skills and understanding through hard work, and that although we may not have enjoyed a subject in the past, we may learn to enjoy it in the future. The difference between the two mindsets looks something like this.

A. Fixed mindset	B. Growth mindset
'I hate maths lessons, because maths lessons have always been a negative experience for me. That means I'll always hate them.'	'I hate maths lessons because I found them difficult. But it's possible I may grow to like them with the right help and some hard work.'
'I'm rubbish at maths. I was born that way. I'll never be any good at it.'	'I've always found maths very difficult. Perhaps it's because it's not been explained to me very well, or I've not paid attention. But with a good teacher and some hard work on my part, I should be able to do better.'

Our challenge as teachers is to move learners from column A to column B. Here is how Loretta Starr would go about it:

> We all know the learners doing retakes come to us struggling under the burden of the Four Big Demotivators as they're scared of English or maths, they're already bored with it and their expectation is that they'll continue being bored with it here, plus their previous experience of it has been a bad one – all about failure and disappointment, and they've already lost all hope of succeeding at it before we even start. So, a bit of the old Razzmatazz is absolutely essential to jolt them out of this four-pronged fixed mindset. I set out to demonstrate to them, right from the start, that their preconceived ideas about the subjects are wrong. I incorporate a lot of English and maths embedded in my vocational classes. I don't try to sneak it in – I flag it up. But I always avoid replicating the sort of 'classroom' teaching style they've experienced at school. I don't stand at the front, writing on the board, for example. I don't give them sheets of uncontextualised 'sums' or grammar exercises. I always incorporate English and maths into activities that are fun, entertaining and designed to hook into their out-of-college interests. This begins to challenge their fixed mindset about English or maths being a) boring, b) always a negative experience and c) always scary.
>
> The Loss of Hope is more complicated to address, particularly in the case of learners who really do struggle, even with the basics. It's no good just vaguely promising they'll get there if they work hard. A better answer, I think, is to break down tasks into small, interesting, enjoyable and achievable steps and to praise individuals enthusiastically for each of those steps forward, however small. This begins to break down that fixed mindset of theirs about having no hope of success. Feed them success. Show them what it feels like.

Putting maths and English to Work

'I haven't come to college to do *schoolwork*. I've come to do painting and decorating!'... or hairdressing, or hospitality and catering, or land-based studies, or sport. You've certainly heard that lament often enough and it's possible that in many ways you can understand it. You probably didn't come into FE to teach English and maths, you came into the profession to pass on your vocational expertise. But that complaint of the learner's can, with a bit of ingenuity, be taken as an opportunity to build up their motivation, because English and maths are, without a doubt, two of the most important transferable skills. They come in useful in any vocation, and some aspect of them will almost always be essential to doing a job well. Learners think of them as school subjects and in their mind there is often a disconnect between the world of school and the world of work. So they don't see the relevance of English and maths to the 'real world'. This is particularly a problem when all the emphasis has been on *achieving the qualification at grade A to C, rather than on the long-term usefulness of the skills and knowledge needed to do that.* The challenge for teachers in FE is to turn that on its head.

Amy Harman, that great exponent of Rules and Respect (see Chapter 4) has, not surprisingly, a set of rules to offer us about making the retakes relevant to the learners' needs, whether you are embedding or teaching separate classes for English or maths:

Do	Don't
Always contextualise tasks and exercises in the learners' chosen vocational area. So if they're calculating area, for example, land-based learners should be working out the area of a field/greenhouse/lawn. If it's an English comprehension practice, use a recipe for catering learners, a sporting report for sports learners and so on.	Set tasks that are simply academic exercises, or where the context bears no relation to the world of work. This will only remind them of school.
Use examples that are taken from the world of work: 'If you need to calculate proportions for a colour mix. . .', 'If you're filling in a work report for your boss. . .'	Use examples that harp on about the exam: 'If you get this in the exam. . .' and so on. This just takes them right back to school.
Encourage their interest and grab their attention by telling them an anecdote from the world of work, possibly something from your own experience, which involves the use or misuse of the aspect of English or maths you're about to introduce them to.	Justify each topic by saying, 'You'll need this to pass the exam.' This suggests it's ALL they'll need it for – which is just not true (and a compete turn-off).
Invite in one or two past learners, preferably those you are young, who are now successfully employed in that vocational area and invite the class to ask them how they are applying their English and maths skills day-by-day at work. This needs some careful briefing and preparation, but it'll be worth it.	Ask an employer to come in and tell them how important it is to have a good GCSE in English and maths. They'll have been told this 100 times. If it hasn't motivated them before, it's unlikely to now.

How are the teachers coping?

It's probably occurred to you as you've reading through this chapter that it's not only the learners who've been feeling demotivated at the thought of these re-sits, it's many of the teachers as well, which is not surprising. Teachers, too, may have qualms about English and maths. They may be worried their own skills aren't up to teaching or embedding these subjects; after all, they never signed up to be English or maths teachers. Their own previous experience of studying these subjects may not even be a positive one and they possibly worry that they won't be able to teach them effectively. There's also the question of having to cope with unmotivated, disengaged and possibly, as a result, disruptive learners. That's three of the Four Big Demotivators that teachers may have to struggle with themselves before they even begin to think about motivating the people they're teaching. (Although at least they're not suffering Boredom. How could you ever have time to be bored when you're teaching in FE?) So, while every chapter in this book offers strategies that will be helpful to teachers who have these concerns, at the end a short postscript looks specifically at ways to keep motivated yourself.

Summary

In this chapter we've explored the specific challenges faced when teaching English and maths resits in FE. We've recognised that all four of the Big Demotivators – Fear, Boredom, Previous Negative Experience and Loss of Hope – will need to be addressed and this means that all the motivational strategies described in Chapters 2 to 5 will need to be brought into play. But, in addition to these, we now have a range of ideas and approaches for specifically improving the motivation of these resit groups. Let's summarise them here:

- Spend some time helping learners to find out for themselves what a good GCSE in English or maths *can do for them* in terms of opportunities and progression routes. This shifts them away from the notion that the only reason they'd have for doing it is because the college or the government (or you!) say so.
- Consider renaming or 'rebranding' the subject when you and the learners are talking about it informally. This emphasises a fresh start and a clean break from the negative feelings they attach to the school subject. The example we saw was to rebrand maths as 'The Numbers Game'. Another one that's worked well between learners and teacher is to rename English as 'Language for Winners'.
- Invite in carefully chosen successful learners from a previous year and let them explain to your current learners how they started out with all the same fears

and reluctance but succeeded in the end. This demonstrates that it can be done and they'll be persuaded by peers more readily than they'll be persuaded by you.

- Challenge their fixed mindset that English and/or maths are too difficult and/ or too boring, and help them to develop a growth mindset instead. Do this by introducing fun and enjoyment into lessons where they never expected to find them and planning for them to experience successive small steps of achievement so that they can no longer claim, 'I can't do this.'
- Avoid replicating 'classroom' teaching styles, which will be familiar to the learners from their experience at school. This might include avoiding too much standing at the front and writing on the board, for example. Instead, plan activities and tasks that are fun to do and learner-friendly.
- Make sure you consistently emphasise the relevance of the component skills of English and maths to the world of work. They've heard enough when they were at school about the need to achieve the qualifications at grade A to C. They can dismiss this as what the school or the government want. Now that they're vocational learners they'll respond much better to hearing about the long-term usefulness to them of the skills and knowledge these subjects will give them.

10 Talking the talk: challenging the language of demotivation

Learners and losers: changing definitions

When your 14–19-year-old learners talk about classmates who show a willingness or enthusiasm for learning, what sort of words do they use? Two recent favourites have been:

- **Try'ard** – used to describe someone who's clever or who gets on with work or – at a minimum – answers a question in class.

- **Loser** – used to describe anyone whose attitude to learning seems to coincide with that of the teacher.

No young learner wants to have peers tagging him or her with labels like these. Peer pressure exerted in this way – forming attitudes to learning through the colonisation and subversion of the language used to describe it – is very powerful. The insidious effects of this language of demotivation are very difficult for us, as teachers, to address. But we do need to challenge it, and this first part of the chapter looks at ways in which we might do that.

There's a contradiction, of course, inherent in the way these terms have been coined or applied. A **Try'ard** is someone who is being mocked and goaded for doing precisely what it is we want our learners to do; trying hard. So this term of abuse strikes directly at the heart of all our efforts to get our learners motivated. If they try hard they become a **Try'ard**. This is difficult stuff to deal with. **Loser**, on the other hand, is a term we might think most applicable to someone who chooses to waste their learning opportunities. But no. It's commonly used as an insult to hurl at someone who is interested and motivated. The fact that both these terms have become subverted is a measure of the underlying attitude of disengagement. But it also demonstrates the power of language, a power we ourselves can harness for the purpose of getting learners engaged again.

Language and attitude

What the pejorative use of terms like those above illustrates nicely is that:

- Our attitudes will shape our language. ('We don't like learning so we call someone who learns a "loser".')

- Language will shape our attitudes. ('We don't want our peers calling us a "loser", so we avoid engaging with the learning.')

For the teacher who is attempting to get learners motivated, this is the double whammy.

And of course, this link between language and attitude applies equally to ourselves as teachers. Our attitude to the learners – while not overtly expressed – may be implicit in some of the language we use. If the way we think shapes the way we choose to express ourselves, then what do we make of this conversation between two teachers we've met before: Sly Cunningham and Loretta Starr?

Sly: Most learners can be motivated in the end. It's just a question of finding what works best, the carrot or the stick.

Loretta: Well, it's been a battle to get this lot motivated, but at least now I think I'm winning.

In Sly's comment, learners are being cast in the role of donkeys or some other stubborn animal with a name for being stupid; and in Loretta's reply the teacher–learner interface is seen as a battleground where the victory of one will be won at the cost of defeat for the other. Clearly neither of these constructs is a useful way of thinking about the roles of teacher and learner; and those two teachers would probably be horrified if it was assumed that these were a literal expression of their view. Nevertheless, because of the way that language works, the way that we say things can both reflect and make an impact upon the way we think. If we look at Loretta's statement again – 'It's a battle to get this lot motivated, but at least now I think I'm winning' – we see that it reflects a fairly common construct' of the learning process as being a sort of war between teacher and learners. We often hear related expressions such as, 'I'm gaining some ground', or 'It's been a struggle to get them to do their assignment', or 'I'm not going to let them beat me.' But construing the process of motivating learners as a conflict situation is in the end counter-productive, because the ultimate goal – the learner's successful completion of the task or course or qualification – is in fact a shared victory, won by learner and teacher together. When it comes down to it there really is no conflict of interest.

So how are we going to use language to get away from such implicit ideas that unmotivated learners are stubborn individuals to be prodded or tempted, or armed hostiles to be faced down and defeated? One of the ways is through use of that word itself: **Learner**. It's used consistently throughout this book, in preference to **student** or **trainee**, and – as we saw in the introduction – there's a reason for that. Educational research has shown that teacher expectations can create self-fulfilling prophecies. If we treat learners as though they are poor performers and talk about them (and particularly to them) in those terms, they will usually live up – or perhaps we should say 'down' – to those expectations. But if we demonstrate that we have, within a realistic scale, high expectations of them, learners are more likely to try harder and succeed. By referring to them as 'learners' we are not only naming the purpose for which they are in FE, but also making clear our primary view of them, and exactly what it is we expect of them.

Emphasising the shared goal

Another strategy is to use language that emphasises the shared goal. This can be as simple, for example, as 'Come on, *we* can do this', instead of 'Come on, *you* can do this', or 'If *we* get this done we can have a break.' It can also be addressed by using the language of negotiation rather than the language of command ('How about if we. . ', rather than 'Get on with what I've told you to do. . '). All this may seem simplistic, but the words you choose – the words the learners hear – signal how you feel about them and shape how they feel about themselves. So it's worth choosing those words carefully.

Reclaiming the language

As for how we make it cool to be a Try'ard, this will depend very much on how we respond to that kind of language. Rather than try to fight or forbid or contradict, it's a good idea to point out now and again some role-models who – while being undeniably bright, motivated, hard-working and academically inclined – nevertheless have a high level of credibility in current youth culture. This would apply, for example, to assorted celebs, footballers, other sports personalities and rock stars who've enjoyed success in their education and training and are reported as saying so. Hammer this home at every opportunity and pin it up on the wall if necessary:

- It's cool to succeed.
- The world is divided into Losers and Learners. Which do you want to be?

How language frames the teacher's role

But it's not only the learners who become defined and constrained by the language used to describe them. Teachers, too, have found their role redefined by terms such as **deliver**. We speak of teachers **delivering** a lesson, or of a college **delivering** a curriculum. Taken at face value, this reduces the teacher's role in the learning process from that of instigator and creative facilitator to that of a go-between or messenger who presents the learners with a course or lesson content that has originated elsewhere and been fashioned by someone else, somewhere else, without that specific group of learners in mind. This disempowering, 'teacher-lite' construct of our role does us no favours at all when it comes to the task of motivating learners. How do we build up Relationships, responding to individual needs when we only **deliver** the lesson? How do we create a Culture of Respect, or plan creatively in order to inject a bit of Razzmatazz? And, perhaps most important of all, how does the idea of yourself as someone who just **delivers** – as opposed to **creates, manages, facilitates, inspires** – affect your motivation? The figurative language we use can have more far-reaching implications than we might bargain for. The key here is to:

- Listen to the words and expressions you use about teaching and learning. What do they say about your beliefs and attitudes?
- Think carefully about what you say and how you say it, *before* you say it!

Clear communication

We've looked at how the language we use in talking to and about our learners can reflect and shape how we relate to them and they to us. In this section we're going to look at how to use clear communication to overcome potential barriers to learners' motivation.

Here's what Mo has to say about his teacher:

You know that cartoon? The one with the dog? And the owner's talking away to him, telling him they're going for a walk and they're going to throw some sticks and walk by the pond and all that stuff. And what the dog's hearing is, 'Blah blah blah blah walk. Blah blah blah blah sticks. Blah blah blah.' Well, that's what it's like in Mr R's class. He's going on and on, and nobody can understand what he's on about. But if you ask him anything he looks at you like you're stupid, and he goes, 'We've got to get on with this. We've got a lot to get through,' and all that. So we just don't bother. We just piss about. No point, innit?

Now, obviously none of us likes to think we do this. But the trouble is, it's so easily done. There are whole swathes of our vocabulary and general knowledge that we take for granted, and it's all too easy to think we're communicating when in fact we're doing the very opposite. And, as Mo's comments illustrate, the immediate effect of this is to switch learners off. This isn't to say that we shouldn't introduce learners to a wider vocabulary; that's part of what learning's about. And with some subjects it's difficult to communicate ideas clearly without first becoming familiar with a specialised vocabulary. Some useful pointers here are:

- Start from where the learners are in terms of vocabulary, and build up gradually from there.

- When introducing a word or phrase that you think might be unfamiliar to them, check it out with them: 'Anybody tell me what this means?' or – if you don't want to expose anyone as a try'ard – 'Some of you may know this already, but this means. . .'

- Find alternative ways of saying something. Say it one way; then phrase it in a different way. And then, if you really want to be sure, ask some questions to ascertain whether they've 'got it'.

- Remember that even when there seems to be a general understanding, there may still be some learners who are making neither head nor tail of what you're saying. While you can't always proceed at the pace of the slowest learner, you'll need to find a way to bring everyone on board that avoids singling someone out in front of others, otherwise the slowest learner will lose motivation altogether. The best way is usually a one-to-one explanation, as and when necessary, as you go from learner to learner overseeing and assessing a task.

- Where specialised vocational vocabulary is used, provide a glossary of terms, make sure they've all got a copy, and refer to it frequently. Once learners can talk the talk they'll feel more motivated and empowered to walk the walk.

- Every time you use a word, name or phrase that might be unfamiliar to the learners, write it on the board. This is particularly helpful to those who learn best by seeing things written down. But the key point here is that by writing it on the board you signal that this is important and should be noted down. Such cues are essential for learners who – like many 14–19-year-olds – lack note-taking skills.

The language of learners

One of our roles as FE teacher, whatever our subject area, is to equip learners with communication skills that will serve them well in the adult world of work, to encourage their ability to distinguish between formal and informal modes of speech and to judge when one is more appropriate than the other. The idea that some occasions or interactions call for a more formal manner of speech than they would habitually use with their family or peers is often a difficult concept for younger learners to grasp. What's the best response, for example, when Winnie offers the following contribution to a class discussion on anti-social behaviour?

'We seen that happening once when we was down town. There was these two fit lads, right, and they was having a scrap and one of them were getting well hotted up and I was like, "No way. Let's bail." And my mate, right, she's like a right diva and she's like, "Hang about. This is sick. . ."'

Do you:

1 Thank Winnie for her contribution and move quickly on?

2 Thank Winnie for her contribution and ask her to run through it again for your benefit, explaining some of the more esoteric usages?

3 Announce that you didn't understand a word of what Winnie was saying and tell her to speak properly?

4 Thank Winnie for her contribution and open up some of the points she's making (violence on the street, fights as a spectator sport) for wider discussion?

5 Say, 'Er, quite', and make a mental note to look stuff up in your dictionary of modern slang?

The serious point here is that if you challenge or correct learners every time they open their mouth they're going to stop contributing altogether. The fact that Winnie has chosen to weigh in with an anecdote of her own means that she's feeling sufficiently motivated to engage with the lesson. So it could be entirely counter-productive if you respond to that by immediately correcting her grammar. On the other hand, you have an ideal learning opportunity here for enabling the learners to identify some of the differences between formal and informal speech. So the approach you'd probably choose would be a combination of 2 and 4. Rewarding Winnie by accepting and using her contribution will keep her motivated, as will the sense of being valued for herself and her experience. Asking for some clarification for your own benefit provides the class with an opportunity to turn the tables and teach *you* something. A chance to teach the teacher is difficult to resist and if this is handled with good humour it could draw in even the hardest to motivate. This tactic allows the learners to consider two versions of the same account, and consider which would be used when.

As for usages that would be formally identified as grammatical 'errors' (the 'we was' and 'I aren't' of colloquial speech), again it's obviously counter-productive to be correcting them at every turn. A more effective approach is simply to ensure you always model correct usage yourself when the formality of the situation demands it.

Giving instructions

As teachers one thing we find ourselves doing a lot of is telling learners what to do. We can optimise our chances of their compliance if we phrase our instructions in certain ways. For example, compare these ways of explaining to learners what they should do:

Teacher A says. . .	Teacher B says. . .
1. Get your files out.	1. What I'd like you to do now is to get your files out.
2. Save your work and turn your machines off and put your stuff away and turn to face me now.	2. It's time now to save your work. I'm going to give you 60 seconds to make sure all your work is saved, and your machine shut down, and I'm going to begin counting down. . .NOW . .3. . .2. . .1. . .0. Good. Thank you. Now, I want you all to turn and face me.
3. Get into groups of three. Quietly!	3. I'm going to count you off now into groups of three, so listen carefully so that you know who you're working with.
4. You! And you! Sit down! Now!	4. Okay. Jo? Benji? What I'd like you to do is to sit down now, please.
5. If you're going to do that you can get out. Go on. Get out of the room. Get out now!	5. That's not appropriate behaviour for the classroom. I'd like you to stop doing that now. Or, if you prefer, you can carry on with it, but outside, please.

Teacher B's approach usually stands more chance of success. Let's have a look at why.

1   Teacher B's 'What I'd like you to do now is to get your files out' has a number of advantages over Teacher A's blunt order to 'Get your files out'.

   i) It's polite, whereas Teacher A's approach is rude and doesn't model even the minimum level of politeness you'd hope to encourage in the learners.

   ii) It is phrased as a request and is therefore less confrontational.

   iii) It strikes a positive note. Getting their files out is something the teacher would *like* them to do – suggesting both that here's an easy way to please the teacher and that the teacher is enthusiastic about being there.

2   Teacher A's instruction is too long a string of orders: 'Save your work and turn your machines off and put your stuff away and turn to face me now'. It's also asking something impossible, because the learners won't be able to carry out the first three instructions quickly enough to obey the fourth: 'now'. So they'll probably not bother doing any of them, or at least not the last one. Teacher B's approach is more likely to work because:

   i) She flags up a warning that she's about to give the instruction to 'save'.

ii) She specifies a timescale that's realistic while at the same time being sufficiently tight to promote a sense of urgency.

iii) She uses the countdown again to lend urgency to the task, but also to inject a bit of fun.

iv) She cuts out the 'stuff away' instruction because they can do that at the end.

v) She allows them to complete the first instruction – and praises them – before issuing the next one.

vi) Again she models the sort of clear and polite communication she wishes to encourage in the learners.

3 Teacher A's blunt order is a recipe for chaos: 'Get into groups of three. Quietly!' We only have to close our eyes to imagine the noise and chaos that ensued. Teacher B, on the other hand:

i) avoids providing learners with such an opportunity to mill around, argue, delay, isolate or exclude members of the group

ii) numbers them off – an activity that in itself can create some calm because it calls for learners to listen – and uses (apparently) random grouping, so that although she denies the learners a choice of whom to work with, she doesn't appear to be choosing for them

iii) asks them to listen carefully, instead of telling them to be quiet.

In motivational terms there's a big difference there.

4 Getting learners to sit down can be a constant struggle. Teacher A here is issuing orders, as usual. She'll probably have less success with this than Teacher B, for reasons we can see more clearly if we break down what Teacher B says:

i) 'Okay'– She starts with a positive. This sends a number of signals, including, 'I'm feeling perfectly comfortable', and 'I quite like being here teaching you', and 'I'm not getting stressed about this, so there's no point pushing me to see what happens.'

ii) 'Jo? Benji?' – She uses the learners' names (we'll be saying more about this in the next section). This serves two purposes: it attracts their attention and it plays the Relationship card. And if you're trying to model appropriate behaviour, it is also much more polite than 'You!'

iii) 'What I'd like you to do. . .'– As in number 1, giving an instruction in terms of what you would like the learners to do is a way of emphasising both the relationship and the positive aspect of this particular interaction.

It also flags up that you're about to ask them to do something, and it allows you to SMILE while you say it.

iv) '. . . is to sit down now, please.' – This models politeness. It is clear as an instruction, but is phrased as a request and so is non-confrontational. Nevertheless, it is firm and specific, signalling that they should comply immediately.

5 We've seen that Teacher B avoids being confrontational. She does this with good reason, as Teacher A's approach here will illustrate. We don't know what the learner is doing here. Let's assume he's reading a magazine or playing on his phone. (If, on the other hand, he's waving an offensive weapon or selling a Class A drug, we're dealing with something more than motivational issues and might have more sympathy for Teacher A's outburst.) Teacher A issues three direct orders: 'Go on. Get out of the room. Get out now!' Now, the trouble with direct orders from FE teachers is that they're not likely to receive immediate back-up. So if you tell the learner to 'Get out now!' and he refuses, all you've succeeded in doing is escalating the situation. Instead of having a learner playing a game, you've got a learner bristling with defiance, daring you to chuck him out, with all the rest of the class as a delighted audience looking on. Teacher B's approach won't always succeed, but it will sometimes, and is much less likely to turn a motivational problem into a behavioural one.

i) First, she makes it clear that this not something personal; it's about rules and respect: 'That's not appropriate behaviour for the classroom.'

ii) Then she phrases the instruction clearly as a request: 'I'd like you to stop doing that now.'

iii) Next she models positive, polite interaction – the attitude she would like the learner to adopt in responding: 'Or, if you prefer . . .'

iv) She provides a choice: 'you can carry on with it, but outside, please.'
The learner is not made to feel disempowered. This again establishes that the issue is about rules and respect and is in no way personal. This last point is emphasised by the tone of the request, which, even on the page, can be seen to be calm and measured. The teacher is saying: 'You haven't made me cross. There's no fun to be had pushing this one. I'm not going to lose my temper.'

And if he just carries on with his game? Well, unfortunately Teacher B's approach won't always work. But in most situations it's more likely to have a positive effect on learner motivation than Teacher A's more peremptory style. We'll go back to that game or magazine, or whatever the problem was, in Chapter 11, and consider what we might do if the learner does carry on despite Teachers A and B's best efforts.

What's in a name?

We've suggested in the previous section that use of learners' names can have an impact on their motivation. You'll find it much more difficult to motivate your learners if you don't call them by name, or can't because you don't know what their names are. But it's no good knowing just a few names – the ones you're always having to sort out or persuade to join in – because that only reinforces the idea that learners will gain your attention and make themselves worth knowing by *not* cooperating or working. This is quite the opposite of the effect you're trying for. Some useful guidelines are:

- Learn all the learners' names as early as possible.

- Use them at every opportunity (this also helps you remember them).

- Use them when you're giving praise as well as when you're giving instructions.

- Use the version the learner is most comfortable with. (For example, if a learner prefers to be known as 'Baz', don't ruin his street cred by calling him 'Basil' all the time. That's not the way to get him motivated.)

- On the other hand, don't use a name that's reserved for his mates' use only. (Calling him 'The Bazster' will only embarrass him, not to mention yourself.)

- You'll also have to consider your use of collective nouns when addressing the class as a whole. 'Listen up, you lot' is less effective than 'Listen up, people', or 'Listen up, folks', or 'Listen up, guys', for all the obvious reasons: it's less polite; it's demeaning; it suggests a faceless mob rather than a group of individuals. You may even like to try 'Ladies and Gentlemen'. Some teachers – unlikely as it sounds – have used that mode of address on the grounds that it demonstrates respect and positive expectations, and have claimed that it's successful – not just with adult learners, either.

And then, of course, you have to decide what you'd like the learners to call you. Assuming you have a choice.

Body language

Finally, we're going to consider a language that is central to our success as teachers, one that most learners are already able to read and interpret with great fluency. A teacher's body language can have an enormous effect on learner behaviour and to do the topic full justice would take far more space than this book allows. So we'll look briefly here at five essential ways in which you can use your body language to get learners motivated and keep them that way.

1   **Act enthusiastic**. You can't expect learners to feel any enthusiasm for a lesson if teachers adopt the sort of body language that makes them look as though they're waiting to be beamed up or put out of their misery. So use wide, expansive gestures; keep your expression mobile, your eyes twinkling. Stand up. Forget all that advice about not waving your hands about. Waving your hands about is what you do when you're enthusiastic. That, and smiling a lot.

2   **Don't look nervous**. Looking nervous is catching. If you look nervous, the learners will pick it up and react in a number of possible ways, none of them positive. So how do you stop yourself looking nervous? Get out from behind that desk. If your legs feel wobbly, sit on the edge of the desk. Un-hunch those shoulders; unclench those hands; make lots of eye-contact; smile a lot. The more confident you act, the more confident you'll start to feel – as any psychologist will tell you.

3   **Look as if you like them.** You probably do, up to a point. But if you don't, here's how not to let them know it. Get out from behind that desk again. Uncross your arms. Crossed arms are a defensive gesture. It's something we do when we don't like someone we're talking to, or something we're hearing. The same can apply to crossing your legs, and you can double that if you're crossing them at the ankle as well as the knee; so if you're sitting with your legs visible to the class, uncross them so as not to appear defensive. And it's a really bad idea to stand with your legs crossed, because that just looks as if you need the toilet. Nod a lot. Gentle nodding is best (you don't want to look as though your last job was on the back window ledge of a Ford Fiesta). Nod for positive emphasis when you make an important point; but most importantly nod when you're listening to learner responses or questions. The nodding is telling them that you value what they're saying, and that you value them as learners. And – yes, you guessed it – smile a lot.

4   **Get moving.** Moving about the classroom or workshop works very well with 1–3 above. It can demonstrate enthusiasm, signal that you're in control, and show that you like the learners and are happy to join in with different groups or engage one-to-one. We're talking here about purposeful movement, of course – not the sort of pacing up and down of a terminally depressed polar bear. The idea is not to present a moving target, but to engage with the learners by breaking down that idea of separate spaces for teacher and learners. It can also work well to keep learners on task if you move over in their direction in a purposeful manner. But don't get too close (see point 5). The key to moving about in order to motivate learners is to keep your movements unpredictable. Too much regular pacing is likely to have a detrimental effect on learners' ability to stay awake.

5   **Don't be a space-invader**. When you do move over in a learner's direction, keep a smile on your face and never, ever, invade their space. To do so could only be construed as threatening, and would be detrimental to the learner's motivation. Personal safety zones can differ from individual to individual. An arm's length would be a useful rough guide.

Summary

In this chapter we've made the following key points:

- Our choice of language reflects and shapes how we relate to learners and they to us.
- Clear communication, particularly of unfamiliar words and terminology, is essential to learner motivation.
- We need to equip learners with appropriate communication skills without demotivating them through over-correction.
- The way in which we give instructions will affect learners' responses.
- The use of names can play an important role in motivation.
- We can improve and reinforce learners' motivation by the body language we use.

11 What would you do if...?

This chapter presents ten scenarios that will be recognisable to most teachers in FE. In each one there is an issue about learner motivation that needs to be addressed. There will, of course, be no one right answer to any of these; but there are certainly tactics that will normally work better than others. You might like to decide what approach you would use in each instance, given the information you have. Working through this chapter is rather like being confronted with a group you've never taught before, encountering problems with motivation, and having to play things by ear. It's a useful way of considering for yourself where and how you might apply some of the suggestions and strategies set out in the preceding chapters.

Each scenario is followed by a series of questions which may help inform your decision. In the second part of the chapter you'll find suggestions about which might be the best strategy to adopt in each case, and why.

Scenarios

1. What do you do if the learner refuses to comply?

You're explaining an important point to the class, using the data projector to summarise what you're saying and to help them to take down notes. Most learners are copying the points down, some are sprawling about not bothering and one learner is playing a game quite openly on his phone. You tell him to put it away and listen to what you're saying, but he just carries on. Unfortunately, your remonstration has drawn other learners' attention to what he's doing, so you want to resolve this now as quickly as possible. You say, 'Brendan, I want you to put that away now. If you want to carry on playing a game you'll have do it somewhere else.'

Without taking his eyes from the game, Brendan says, 'Yeah. I've nearly finished this level. Whoa! Yeah! Result!'

You say, 'Okay, Brendan. That's it. Take that game somewhere else.'

But Brendan just shakes his head and says, 'No. I'll stay here thanks.'

Some questions to consider before deciding your strategy

- Whose motivation is at stake here (besides your own)?

- Faced with the same situation again, would you consider tactically ignoring what Brendan is doing?

- How do you prevent this problem from escalating into an issue about confrontational behaviour?

2. What do you do if learners don't turn up on time and wander in late in ones and twos throughout the first half-hour of the lesson?

We promised in Chapter 2 that we'd revisit Sly and see how he was getting on with the Group from Hell. He seems to have had some long-term success in getting them motivated, but there are still problems with punctuality. The lesson starts at 11am, but by 11.10 only two-thirds of the class have arrived. This is disastrous for Sly's lesson plan, because today's session should be a demonstration of procedure by him, followed by a practical session where the learners practise the procedure themselves. If Sly starts the demo before they're all here, the latecomers won't be able to benefit from the activity in the second half of the lesson; but if he waits much longer, he'll have to abandon the lesson plan because there won't be time for both demo and practical.

Some questions to consider before deciding your strategy

- What are the immediate and practical motivational issues here?

- What longer-term strategy might Sly employ to avoid this happening in the future?

3. What do you do to stop learners texting when they should be working?

You've set the learners a task from their assignment to do in class because that way you stand a better chance of seeing the work completed. You're moving from table to table, giving help where it's needed. The group you're working with at any one time remain on-task while you're with them; but you've noticed that when you're not directly supervising them, several of the learners have their phones out, which is against college rules. Now and again you hear the vibrating buzz of a phone on silent, so you've worked out that they're texting each other. Although you consider it a bit of a bonus that they're doing this covertly rather than in your face, you know you've got to not only uphold rules but also motivate them to keep on-task otherwise they risk failing this assignment.

Some questions to consider before deciding your strategy

- What exactly are the college rules about phones in the classroom?

- Is there a way to harness the enthusiasm for texting and use it as a motivator for getting the task done?

4. What do you do if learners are misusing the internet in an IT class?

You're teaching a session in an IT room and each learner has his or her own machine. These are arranged in a 'horseshoe' around three walls, with your table and the whiteboard facing the open end. This means that when the learners are using the computers they're seated with their backs to you. You've briefed them for a task that requires them to do some research, and so they're now supposed to be using the computers to access specific sites on the internet that you've detailed for them, and find the information they need. They all seem to be fairly well-occupied; but when you start walking around and looking over their shoulders you find that only about half the class are on-task. The other learners are either accessing websites and material that have nothing to do with the topic in question, or else they're playing online games. You wonder at first whether perhaps they've already completed the task and are amusing themselves until the rest catch up. But when you check, it's clear that they've done no work at all.

Some questions to consider before deciding your strategy

- What's the motivational issue here?

- Is the activity of the off-task learners likely to affect the motivation of those who are getting on with the task in hand?

- Is there a way you can channel this off-task energy and enthusiasm?

5. What do you do when learners are underachieving?

You're teaching a Level 2 class in which there are some learners who are really struggling to reach the required standard in their assessed work. However, there are also two learners in this group who are clearly coasting. They do the bare minimum of work, but what they do complete is of a very good standard. On some tasks they're achieving at Level 3. But they make so little effort on other tasks that their overall attainment level is no better than that of the learners who are struggling. In class they mess around, turn up late, and frequently don't turn up at all. They have failed to hand in their most recent assignment and are in danger of failing the course. How do you motivate them to get on board and begin to realise their potential?

Some questions to consider before deciding your strategy

- How much time and effort do you consider it reasonable to put in to helping two learners out of a group of 18?

- What is the pay-off for these two learners – if any – for not trying to achieve in line with their potential?

6. What do you do when key players don't turn up for group presentations?

You've planned a lesson around four groups of five learners making presentations on the given topic, which they have researched and worked on in their groups for the last two weeks. At the start of the lesson it becomes clear that a number of key players are missing. In group 1, the learner who had been putting the finishing touches to the presentation, and who has the only copy on a USB, has not turned up. In group 2, the first speaker is absent. In group 3, two people are missing, along with all the notes for the presentation. Only group 4 are all present, but in the agreed batting order they had elected to go last, and are reluctant to suddenly step to the front of the queue. These group presentations carry 30 per cent of the marks for the learners' current assignment. What do you do?

Some questions to consider before deciding your strategy

- At the time you're faced with this situation, who do you need to motivate (apart from yourself!)?

- As well as your immediate tactics for resolving the situation, what might your longer-term strategy be to ensure this doesn't happen again?

7. What do you do when an adult learner makes a phone call instead of joining in with a group discussion?

You've just gone through quite a complicated topic with a group of adult learners. You're now going to follow it up with discussion in three small groups, and then get everyone together for a whole-group debrief and some question-and-answer sessions. They all settle into their groups and there's a buzz of interested, on-task discussion going. In one of the groups, however, a learner is sitting chatting on her phone while the discussion goes on around her. At first you wonder whether it's some emergency at home; but it goes on for some time and she's smiling and looking perfectly cheerful, so you assume not. She's getting indignant looks from some of the other learners, and heads are turning to see whether you've noticed it's going on. How do you get her motivated to abandon her phone conversation and join in the discussion?

Some questions for you to consider before deciding your strategy

- Will her adult status be a factor in your choice of tactics?

- Is there a college rule about phones?

- Have you personally negotiated a rule about phones with these particular learners?

- Whose motivation is an issue here?

8. What do you do when learners don't meet the deadline for handing in their assignment?

This is Davit's class. We met them in Chapter 3. We were left wondering whether they would, in fact, complete and submit their assignment. Well, Davit's approach has had some limited success, and they all handed their assignment in by the new deadline. This other teacher, however, is having less luck. He's told this group of learners over and over again that they have to pass this assignment to pass the course and they have to pass the course to get their qualification. He's told them that the next lesson is the absolute deadline for hand-in and it can't be extended because the external verifier's visit is next week. He arrives at the lesson to find that only three out of the 12 learners have brought their assignment to hand in. He expresses his incredulity. He expresses his disappointment. These are met with mutters of 'Whatever', and 'So?' What would you do?

Some questions for you to consider before deciding your strategy

- This is another of those issues that it would take the whole book to do justice to, but one of the questions you could answer for yourself quite quickly here is: if the learners can't be bothered, why are you bothered?

- And can you use to your advantage the fact that you are bothered?

9. What do you do when learners are talking while you're talking?

You're used to teaching against an ongoing background murmur. (Ofsted might even call it 'low level disruption'.) But with this class it's much worse than that. You find you're having to raise your voice just to make yourself heard. You keep repeating those favourite phrases 'Settle down, please!' and 'Keep the noise down, please!' But it's not having any effect. You can see it's bothering the more enthusiastic learners, because they're clearly straining to hear what you say. They constitute about one in four of the class, and you're feeling bad because you know that they hold you responsible for the fact that they have to try to concentrate against this background hubbub. So what do you do?

Some questions for you to consider before deciding your strategy

- Is there any learning going on in this lesson?

- Might there be another way to put this information across that the talkers will pay more attention to?

10. What do you do when one member of a small group is distracting other learners from the group task?

You've got a class of 16–17-year-olds engaged in group-work. It's noisy, but it's productive noise because all the learners are on task. All, that is, except for one. He's doing his level best to distract the other members of his group by talking about something he's seen on YouTube. When he realises you're listening to him his comments become objectionable and even offensive. He gets up and begins wandering around the workshop, peering over people's shoulders and generally making a nuisance of himself. The other learners seem quite tolerant of him, and keep returning to the task. But he himself is getting no work done at all. How do you motivate him to drop the joker act and address the task?

Some questions to consider before deciding your strategy

- Whose motivation is at stake here?

- What's the learner's pay-off for not getting down to some work?

Suggested strategies

1. What do you do if the learner refuses to comply?

This situation returns us to the incident we explored in Chapter 10. We looked there at the way in which the language we use to challenge the learner can have a positive or negative impact on the learner's motivation to comply. We are faced here with a potential stand-off, which could all too easily escalate from a problem with motivation into an issue about confrontational behaviour. You've asked Brendan to stop his off-task activity and turn his attention to his work, or to leave the room. He has refused to do either. So whose motivation is at stake here?

Well, what started as a problem with one learner's motivation now threatens to affect the motivation of the rest of the class. If they see you're unable to resolve this situation, they will draw the conclusion that refusal to comply has no serious consequences. They may begin asking themselves: 'If he can mess around and get away with it, why shouldn't I?' And potentially there is the additional undermining of motivation that would result from allowing a sense of disorder and loss of control to pervade the lesson.

So in finding a way forward you need a strategy that will, at the same time:

- avoid escalation

- make it clear to other learners that non-compliance has its consequences

- prevent a motivation problem from evolving any further into a behaviour problem.

One way you can achieve this is by presenting Brendan with another choice. It could go – calmly – something like this:

- 'All right. Let me give you another choice. Do as I ask you now, or we'll have to sort this out at the end of the lesson. If we have to sort it out at the end of the lesson, the consequences for you will be much more serious, because what you're doing now is in breach of college rules. So it won't be me you have to deal with. Your choice.' And then turn your attention back to the rest of the class, in the assumption of compliance that we talked about in Chapter 4.

There's a good chance this will work. However, even if it isn't as successful as you might hope in motivating the non-compliant learner, it will preserve the motivation of the other learners by de-escalating the conflict and reassuring them that sanctions do exist to support a safe and orderly learning environment.

Finally, we looked at this question: Faced with the same situation again, would you consider tactically ignoring what Brendan is doing? At first glance this might seem, in principle, a bad idea. However, given the situation of a class where all the learners except for one are sufficiently motivated to get on with their work, might we not think twice about drawing attention to that one's off-task activity? Certainly you have a responsibility to Brendan to do everything you can to encourage him to engage with his learning. But you might well decide to approach this in a different way if a similar incident arose again; for example, by quietly engaging him in a conversation that interests him and draws his attention away from his game; or by finding him a more dynamic role – messenger, observer, time- keeper, rapporteur – in the class activity.

2. What do you do if learners don't turn up on time and wander in late in ones and twos throughout the first half-hour of the lesson?

This is one of those situations that all FE teachers are familiar with. Sometimes we can just about get around the fact that the lesson gets off to a ragged start. But in a situation like this, where the necessary learning activities require the learners to attend the full lesson, it can become a real barrier to effective learning.

So, what are the immediate and practical motivational issues here? When you're on the spot, dealing with the situation, there's nothing you can immediately do about the motivation of the learners who are late or missing; but you do have decisions to make about the learners who *have* turned up on time. Postponing the start of the lesson, or getting off to a messy directionless start, interrupted at intervals by latecomers, is unlikely to motivate the punctual learners to keep up their punctuality. So your immediate and practical concern is with their needs. A good strategy, therefore, is to:

- Start on time with those who are present.

- Tell latecomers as they enter to watch whatever's left of the demonstration and that you'll talk to them afterwards.

- Gather the latecomers as a group (once you've set the punctual learners going on the practical task), and explain that they won't be able to carry out the task themselves because they missed the beginning of the demonstration; but that they can now learn the task from one of their classmates. Pair each latecomer with a punctual learner, to observe the task and make notes.

- Give lots of positive feedback (as you go from learner to learner supervising the task), and lots of praise to the learners who are demonstrating to the latecomers.

- Give the punctual learners a short break or early finish, if feasible, when the task is completed; but keep the latecomers in a group with you to go through and consolidate what they've learned.

You'll no doubt recognise at once the motivational principles on which this strategy is based. As we might expect from Sly, they are mostly to do with Reward.

1 The punctual learners are rewarded for their punctuality. They are made to feel that they are the important ones, the focus of your attention. If you spent fifteen minutes looking at your watch and waiting for the latecomers, this sends the wrong messages about who's important and who's in control.

2 The latecomers don't get rewarded for being late. Their behaviour has failed to exert any power over the start time or over the punctual learners' learning experience. Their arrival gains them the minimum of attention.

3 The punctual learners are rewarded by being publicly credited with knowledge and expertise that the others have forfeited by their lateness. They are trusted with an interesting task to do. Some or all of them are paired with a latecomer in an empowering relationship where they have the higher status.

4 The punctual learners are rewarded with a break or early finish, and have the satisfaction of knowing that the latecomers are not!

5 All these rewards are held up to the latecomers as something they have forfeited this time, but could possibly earn in the future.

All of this might well help to avoid the same situation arising again. But lack of punctuality is so endemic among younger learners in FE that this is something each teacher needs to have long-term strategies for. For example, in schools, at Key Stages 3 and 4, **Starter Activities** are used at the beginning of lessons to get pupils in the right frame of mind for learning. Some of the settling activities we looked at in Chapter 7 adopt this same idea, in a form appropriate for FE.

One additional strategy Sly would probably introduce to address this punctuality problem in the longer term is the **Punctuality Raffle**. All learners who arrive on time get a ticket, the prize is something worth having, and learners can earn additional tickets (i.e. increase their chance of winning) by being punctual all week, handing work in on time, and so on.

3. What do you do to stop learners texting when they should be working?

This is another perennial problem. The way you address it will depend upon whether there is a college policy on the use of mobile phones, *and whether there is a will to enforce it*. It's hard for you to try to enforce college rules as part of your motivational tactics if it's difficult to get support for this in individual cases. If there's a rule and there are clear procedures for the enforcement of it, you can remind the learners of the rule and of the consequences of breaking it. However, the fact that several of them are texting may be an indication that they're not finding the learning task sufficiently engaging. Here are three things you can try in this situation:

1   Gather them as a group and enter into some negotiation about the task. Explore whether there are any non-essential changes that might make it more interesting to them.

2   Gather them together as a group and negotiate a different way to *approach* the task (e.g. could they produce it first in 'text-speak' and then translate it into more formal English?).

3   Make a deal with them that if they get the task satisfactorily completed they can have six minutes' texting time (six minutes sounds a more attractive offer than five). But obviously don't use this one if it contravenes college rules, otherwise next time you try to use Respect or Rules as a motivator, you won't have a leg to stand on.

The idea behind gathering learners as a group to negotiate is that a) it's less confrontational than one-to-one, b) it takes up far less of your valuable teaching time and c) often, learners will abide more readily by a consensus of peers than by a condition 'imposed' by the teacher.

4. What do you do if learners are messing about in an IT class?

One of the characteristics of lessons where every learner is seated at a computer is that individuals can be off-task without other learners knowing anything about it. This means that their lack of engagement is unlikely to affect the motivation of others. And so the motivational issue in this particular scenario is confined to the learners who are accessing the internet for purposes other than those they've been briefed for. Frequently it's the most IT-confident learners who do this. If that's the case, one way you can motivate them to access the sites and the information you want them to is to get them to help out another learner who's finding the task less easy. Or you could get them to act as trouble-shooters, helping out if other learners get stuck. This has the advantage of harnessing their enthusiasm and expertise in a positive and productive way, and also makes them feel valued rather than bored or frustrated. Of course, the drawback of this tactic is that you could end up with twice as many learners off-task. So if you feel that approach is too high risk, you could try introducing differentiation in a more formal way, providing briefings for a series of increasingly advanced activities that learners can work their way through. We're assuming here that the problem is Boredom – or at least lack of suitable challenge.

If, on the other hand, you suspect it's not really a challenge they're after, you could try some variant on the 'every minute wasted is a minute deducted from everybody's break time' approach. This is more effective if you build in a number of very short breaks – particularly where learners are working at computers. The short breaks are an opportunity not only for negotiating reward, but also for getting learners turned away from their screen and making some eye-contact with you.

5. What do you do when learners are underachieving?

This is such an enormous question, we could fill a library and several websites and still not have a reliable answer. In this particular scenario, however, we have a specific motivational problem that has come to an acute head and requires an immediate response because these two learners are in imminent danger of failing the course. We posed the question: 'How much time and effort do you consider it reasonable to put in to helping two learners out of a group of 18?' The answer in this case is probably, 'As much as it takes'. Nevertheless, it's still a serious question which, in less acute circumstances, we might want to ponder quite carefully. As teachers we have a responsibility to motivate and support all our learners. If we are putting a disproportionate amount of time and effort into trying to motivate one or two, we have to be confident that this is not time that's being deducted from supporting, encouraging and enthusing the rest. However, all things being equal, this sort of utilitarian thinking – the good of the many taking precedence over the good of the few – is difficult to view as consistent with the ethical demands of being a teacher.

Some emergency interventions you could try with these two underachievers are:

- Sitting down with them and cheering them on as they write their assignment under your eagle eye – while the rest of the class get on with a structured learning activity. This has the advantage of making the two underachievers feel valued – but may equally make the rest of the learners who did get their work in on time feel badly done by.

- Negotiating with the external verifier to have some of their assessment carried out as a viva or oral exam.

- Give them a final two-day extended deadline. Then allocate each of them a 'buddy' who has already handed the work in to discuss the assignment with them, suggest sources of information, and generally stay on their case until the assignment is handed in. This can be surprisingly effective if you choose the buddy with care.

- Telephone or write politely to their parent/s or carer/s, explaining the seriousness of the situation and asking them to weigh in with some encouragement. (Schools use this approach a lot, so don't worry that carers will think it strange.) This step will usually need to be agreed with your line manager first.

Assuming one of these – or something else – works, you then have some longer-term planning to do. What was the pay-off, from their point of view, for sailing so close to the wind? Well, for a start they certainly got to monopolise the teacher's attention towards the end, didn't they? So it might be a good idea to consider some of the following questions:

- Are you providing differentiated tasks and differentiated assessments to challenge these particular learners and keep them interested?

- Are you giving them enough attention, or is all your attention being focused on helping the learners who are struggling?

- Can you incorporate more time in your lessons for working on assignment tasks in class?

- If so, could you use a different variation of the buddy arrangement and introduce some peer support where the two learners in question are partnered with learners whom they can help?

6. What do you do when key players don't turn up for group presentations?

Although the two scenarios are different, many of the issues here are identical to those discussed in Question 2. The learners who are in immediate need of motivation are those who've turned up. They've put the work in, suffered the prepresentation nerves, and suddenly find their co-learners – purposely or not – have sabotaged their efforts. The group who have all turned up are at risk of being particularly demotivated if the presentations don't go ahead.

Tactics for handling this situation are a little different from those in Question 2. In order to keep up these learners' motivation you need to ensure two things:

1 Their preparations and practice should not be wasted.

2 The absent learners should not be allowed to 'get away with it'.

This means that you'll need to give those who are there part of the lesson to arrange to merge groups or borrow stand-ins from other groups, or to produce the bare minimum of what resources they need – for use with the data projector, for example. This may involve cutting down slightly the time allowed for each presentation. You'll also need to:

- find lots of points about the presentations on which to give positive feedback

- provide lots of praise and encouragement to the learners for a) turning up and b) persevering despite the setback

- make it absolutely clear that those who are absent will still be required to do presentations in order to pass their assignment.

It's possible that one or more of the absentees genuinely couldn't face standing up and presenting. That's another motivational issue you will have to explore and if necessary address. It's important, therefore, not to make the blanket assumption that all those who are absent are 'skiving'; and it's equally important not to talk about them to the other learners in these terms.

7. What do you do when an adult learner makes a phone call instead of joining in with a group discussion?

This caller is getting indignant looks from other learners, which is your clue that there are two motivational problems here:

1 Why does this learner prefer to make a phone call rather than join the learning activity?

2 How can you prevent this behaviour from antagonising and affecting the motivation of the other learners?

So will her adult status be a factor in your choice of tactics? The answer is probably, to some extent, 'Yes'. You've got to be seen to be addressing the issue (see 2 above), but anything that sounds like a reprimand, particularly if issued publicly, is likely to have a negative impact on the learner in question. Here are some possible tactics:

- Take her to one side and remind her about the phone rule. The rest of the learners will notice this, be pleased at your intervention and reassured by your discretion.

- Issue a blanket reminder that all phones should be switched off, without overtly directing it at that particular learner.

- Say to her, 'Oh dear. Is there a problem at home? If there's a problem at home you can take that call in the corridor.'Then follow her into the corridor, ascertain what's going on and remind her – in a non-officious way – of the rules.

8. What do you do when learners don't meet the deadline for handing in their assignment?

Many of the same issues apply here as in the answer to Question 5, except in this case it's the majority, rather than the minority, who fail to hand in their work, and we have no indication here that they are underachievers. However, it's clear that any learner who fails to hand in work and risks failing the course and the qualification has real problems with motivation. That there are so many in this group suggests that there may still be a longer-term need to address issues about some or all of the following:

- selection and recruitment
- the content, design and format of assignments

- the clarity of assignment briefs and deadlines

- the advisability of providing class time for the completion of assignments

- the support and advice given for assignment-writing skills

- the quality and frequency of formative assessment.

In terms of immediate action, the teacher can use to his advantage the fact that he is bothered about these learners and their future. By demonstrating this, he is already acting to motivate them, as well as modelling the appropriate attitude (which is to be *really* bothered!). For specific emergency tactics he might try, see the answer to Question 5.

9. What do you do when learners are talking while you're talking?

Sometimes, in the real world, you can just put up with a bit of background talking. It's irritating; but if it's not creating a barrier to learning for the majority of the class, it's often more constructive to proceed than to tie up half the lesson with trying to enforce silence on the garrulous minority. In this scenario, however, you have no choice but to act, because the noise levels are having a detrimental effect on the motivation of the more willing learners, and you've got to the point where it's impossible for much learning to take place.

Here are some questions to consider:

- Could it be you? Have you listened to yourself? Do you sound enthusiastic/ inspiring/compelling? Well, we all have our off-days. But perhaps there's a more dynamic way to get this information across.

- Have you been talking for too long? Remember, the attention span of young learners can be quite short. Have you been talking for more than five minutes?

- Are you astounding them with attention-grabbing images on the screen? On the board? If not, why not?

- Are you providing signposts – a summary of the main points you are making – on the board or screen?

- Have you flagged up that this is IMPORTANT, and explained (convincingly) why?

- Is there an alternative way to get this information over to them? DVD? Handouts? Online research?

- Are you communicating effectively? Using language they can understand? Avoiding unfamiliar terminology?

- Have you provided gapped handouts so that they have to listen in order to fill in the right word in the right place?

- Have you offered a prize for all correctly completed gapped handouts?

- Have you issued a challenge?: For example, 'I'm going to say something in the next five minutes that involves the name of a footballer/TV programme/celebrity/rock band, and there's a prize for everyone who hears it and writes it down correctly'.?

10. What do you do when one member of a small group is distracting other learners from the group task?

It seems from this scenario that only one learner's motivation is at issue here. The rest of the group are tolerating him without becoming distracted from their task. So what's his pay-off for not getting down to some work? He's not really getting much attention, and he's not succeeding in disrupting others' learning. You should consider the possibility, therefore, that this learner considers the task either too difficult or too easy. But the only way of discovering for sure what's driving him to use these avoidance tactics is to take a few minutes to engage him quietly in conversation. You'll then be in a position to make an informed choice about the best strategy to get this learner re-engaged with learning.

12 Postscript: Keeping yourself motivated

In the introduction we stressed the enormous impact that learners' attitudes can have on teachers' own motivation. Classes and individuals like the ones we've encountered in this book demand an enormous amount of energy and commitment from the teacher, and sometimes the results, in terms of learner motivation, seem to take a long time to appear. And occasionally, it has to be said, their motivation never does improve, despite all our very best efforts. Although we know that in such cases the lack of motivation often arises from factors that are beyond our ability or remit to control, nevertheless such a situation can be frustrating and disheartening. And so it's all too easy, sometimes, to find our own motivation slipping. If this begins to happen, there are things you can do to help you recover your confidence and enthusiasm. Here are a few of them.

- Think of times you've been successful in motivating your learners. What was your biggest success? How did it make you feel?

- Think of the learners whose lives you've changed for the better – by helping them gain the qualifications or the confidence they needed. Make a point of talking to colleagues and friends who make you feel good about yourself and about teaching. Try to avoid getting into long, 'isn't it awful' conversations with people who seem to be terminally demotivated themselves.

- If you've been teaching for a few years, offer to be a mentor to someone coming in new to the profession, or someone needing professional development. This will help you recognise the wealth of skills, wisdom and experience that you've already accumulated as you watch someone else begin to benefit from them.

- If you're quite new to your post (or even if you're not), ask to be provided with a mentor, someone who can help you think through what's happening in your professional practice and help you to regain your enthusiasm.

- Be kind to yourself. Don't feel you've always got to be centre stage with your teaching, especially if you're feeling disappointed or exhausted. Get the learners doing a learning activity that they find fun – playing a 'game' or watching a video, for example. Seeing learners enjoying a lesson will help remind you of the good things about this job.

- Build more, shorter breaks into your lessons.

- Act enthusiastic, even if you don't feel it. There are two good reasons for this. One is that, as we've seen, acting enthusiastic can often make you genuinely feel that way, as learners begin to respond positively. The other is that revealing your own lack of motivation to a class of learners is only going to make things worse, because it's likely to undermine what motivation they have. Sometimes it can even trigger negative behaviour, and that's the last thing you want to deal with when you're coping with a motivational crisis of your own. In business there's a rather gruesome saying: 'When you're swimming with sharks, don't bleed.' As we've all noticed, learners are less likely to give confident and enthusiastic teachers a bad time.

- Try out a new teaching method, a new seating arrangement, a new strategy for getting learners into groups.

- Do your best not to take work home. This is difficult when there's a lot of marking and preparation to do – which is pretty much always. But keeping some space between work and home gives you the opportunity to take a break and recover some of that physical and emotional energy you're expending every day on getting the learners motivated.

- Make sure you're getting something to eat at lunchtime. It's all too common these days for FE teachers to find themselves timetabled with no lunch break. If you don't get something to eat, you'll lose energy and feel less able to cope with the demands of the job.

- Look for ways to inject novelty, impact and enjoyment into your lesson plans. This is an excellent way to re-energise your own commitment to teaching, and to remind yourself why you chose this profession in the first place.

- At the end of each day, think about the best thing that happened – the success of the day, however small. Try not to dwell on the 'failures'. These are just the potential successes of tomorrow.

References and further reading

Ascham, R. (1570; 2008) *The Schoolmaster*. BiblioLife

DfES. (2005) White Paper: *14–19 Education and Skills*. (http://www.educationengland. org.uk/documents/pdfs/2005-white-paper-14–19-education-and-skills.pdf)

Dweck, C. (2012) *Mindset: How you can Fulfil your Potential*. London: Robinson.

Gershon, M. (2016) *How to Develop Growth Mindsets in the Classroom*. Createspace

Handy, C. (1993) Understanding Organisations (4th Edition). London: Penguin

Maslow, A., Webb, D. (2013) *A Theory of Human Motivation*. CreateSpace

Plevin, R. (2016) *Take Control of the Noisy Class*. Carmarthen: Crown House

Rogers, Bill (2015) *Classroom Behaviour* (4th edition). London: SAGE Publications

Rogers, C. R. (1983) *Freedom to Learn for the 80's*. Indianapolis, USA: Merrill

Index